D1083017

MEAT ON THE HOOF

MEAT
ON THE HOOF
The Hidden World of Texas Football

Gary Shaw

St. Martin's Press   New York

AFFILIATED PUBLISHERS: Macmillan & Company, Limited,
London—also at Bombay, Calcutta, Madras and Melbourne—
the Macmillan Company of Canada, Limited, Toronto.

Acknowledgments

I would especially like to thank Leon Mac Hruska for his many hours of poring over the manuscript with me. His suggestions were extremely valuable but his encouragement and feeling for where I was going were even more valuable.

I would also like to thank the following people for having helped make this book: Jay Acton, Sara Simpson, Tom Wolf, Sherry Maloney and Allan Serotta. Also, the four Texas football players who consented to be interviewed and quoted at length in this book.

For

Mandy	Madeline
Glenn	Carolyn
Johnnie	Don
John	Mathew
Linda	Roy

and anyone else who thinks he has to prove himself human.

Introduction

Although I went through the University of Texas on a football scholarship two years ahead of Gary Shaw, there seems to have been no essential changes from what I remember and what is recounted in his book, except that in his years the Fates had spun away some of the gilded fabric of the Texas winning tradition. But that appears to have been set aright in recent years, reaffirming the strength of that tradition and its monocled concentration on itself.

This book deals with what it was like to enter into this immense tradition, where winning football games is a sacrament of such emotional intensity as to rival those of any other religion. But not every young man who was recruited to Texas to play football could quite measure up to the proportions of demigod. Even those who did were not allowed to enjoy a sense of security from it, for they might fall from favor by injury or attitude and be cast into a shade of uncertainty and anxiety until such time, if good fortune smiled, that they might work back into the less inclement graces of the coaching staff.

But for those who didn't work back far enough and for those who couldn't quite fit the necessary measurements in the first place, there was a peripheral life in a certain kind of limbo where much came to pass that would urge you to form silently the question of whether it was worthwhile to go on. Most went on, at least until the question repeated itself too often, but few went on for any love of playing football. That was utopian fancy.

I can remember that question quite well, for I repeated it too often and quit once during a spring training. I remember the times that I was told that no one was either forced to come or to stay in football: we were always "free" to go. So I exercised this freedom, but came back a day later; not for the love of football, however.

It has been said often enough that no one's spirit is free or restrained by virtue of any material chains. Sometimes, the soul might well up in us in protest at our condition, but we look about and see that there are no accommodations for the soul, so we shove it down again—it is a pest, a nuisance; it might embarrass us, might sully the mask we wear, and it might force us to an initiative. For an adolescent who assumes a cherished posture, it is difficult for his soul's breath to depart and leave a slumped figure.

A fine merit of Shaw's book, I think, is the showing forth of this psychological bondage of adolescent athletes to their fond self-images and how easily manipulatable they become as a result, and how they put up with what might otherwise be quite reasonably walked away from. In fact, the tone of this book is more of inquiry and explanation than of anything else. It might seem as though a sacred institution is being attacked and certain persons are being shown in much less than their usual light of adoration; but this is purposeful beyond its being done for its own sake. And, too, it seems that this book was written more in reflection than in a haste to expose foibles. There were five to nine years between the writing and the events written about, and a perspective formed during the interim. Instead of the grinding of an ax, you hear a sharpened edge paring through the layers of experience and memory in the attempt to let light fall on underlying reasons for what had come to pass.

On reading the book, there comes to mind a perennial issue—and a weary one, too, from having been relentlessly swept beneath the carpet's edge. That is the question of why big-time intercollegiate football, with its only apparent values being winningness and championships belongs beneath the rubric of "Education." The concept of education is confusing and ambiguous enough without its being tugged about into more arbitrary shapes so it can, to the satisfaction of certain notables, accommodate college football. While at Texas, I always resisted the assurances that football had a valid educational purpose. The fellow student waiting tables to pay his obligations was no different from me, except that I received more notice (and more hell) for my labors. Maybe I missed those often preached values of collegiate competition, but I feel less deprived than I feel fortunate, for I didn't acquire instead their counterfeits, which were abounding.

When Shaw mentions that there was no "fun" in football as played at Texas, I would have to agree, but I don't think that what we think of as fun is the final purpose of sports. For the participant, sports can be a deeply revealing experience if he can be allowed to compete without fanatical tension, the kind that comes from knowing that every little mistake will be held against him and that losing will have some evilly metaphysical import. There is an intimate kind of agony in competition that constrains us on deeper into ourselves, further until we melt that agony away into an exhausted yet reinspiring euphoria. There is a mystery about ourselves in those moments that we don't really learn but that we experience, the more intense the experience.

This is not exactly what could be called fun, but it was

not necessarily impossible at Texas, although the pressures
to perform heroically were a hindrance. I've always found
that pressure to win, to grade out a certain percentage in
films, to make this or that amount of yards actually was an
obstacle to best performance. I often thought we won at
Texas in spite of ourselves, and consequently, the only
enjoyment came immediately after a game was over, since
the next day you would feel the pressure to win the up-
coming game.

Shaw makes the point that what he has written about
does not exist only at the University of Texas but at other
schools. I would have to think that true. From talking to
various people from other schools over a period of years,
the impression is that differences are only in degree, not
kind. College football is a big business and mustn't be
thought to be too much unlike most big business. But already I have visions of this book being used by representatives of other schools to persuade prospective athletes not
to go to Texas but to their own school instead. That would
seem such a poor act of deception.

George Sauer
San Francisco, Calif.

Contents

MEAT
ON THE HOOF

Getting It Up

*Like a young god. Hercules—something like that. And
the sun, the sun all around him. Remember how he waved
to me? Right up from the field, with the representatives of
three colleges standing by. And the buyers I brought, and
the cheers when he came out—Loman, Loman, Loman!
God almighty, he'll be great yet. A star like that, magnif-
icent, can never really fade away.*

—Arthur Miller
DEATH OF A SALESMAN

Somewhere I could have lost it all, blown it, gone amok. A screaming crazy Texas teenager charging those metal railings and their wooden seats—a football Frankenstein heading for all those Kiwanians and their school principals, leveling all the bankers who built this trembling vault called a stadium, throwing bleeding forearms to seated mamas and papas and thrusting hard metal cleats at smiling pompoms . . . but it was only moments from the kickoff and what I wanted more than anything was to smash the sixteen-year-old boy in front of me.

As I ground my cleats into dirt, Dicky Pearce, our half-back, threw up.

While the band played "Oh Hail Denton High," I could feel the film projector chasing my number 74, and the entire stadium crowd peering through its lens. I knew my shoulder pads were firmly fitted, but I couldn't help feeling they were out of place. I strained to center them by tugging on my jersey. Out of the corner of my eye I could see Denton's huge stadium clock and behind me were the barely heard rumbled growls and feet of my teammates. When the gate opened, all those wooden benches and parents, pompoms and girls, worn helmets and friends, referees and little brothers, coaches and school songs were jammed together and then funneled into my gut.

Glancing at the enemy across the field, I couldn't stop my left shoulder from involuntarily jerking, and I was driven to bump bodies with now forgotten teammates. These collisions straightened my chest and seemed to keep something locked in my sockets. This was always the

2

worst part—before our initial contact with our "real" enemy. Then I could put it on automatic, and it was only by hitting in a game that all the jumping and jerking and growling and running and pulling of my gut could get some kind of relief.

"But I don't think I can make it."

"Gary, you can do anything if you want it bad enough, but you can't hold back and get it. Now have you really been giving it your best? Have you really been doing everything you can out there?"

I shook my head no.

Now I was an eighth grader, weighing one-hundred-thirty pounds. I didn't like workouts, I didn't like to get hit, I was not very aggressive, and after each game I felt whittled down another notch. I was one of only two players who never got into a game, and afterwards, I would hide in my bedroom and cry, a failure for life at thirteen. And by the middle of the season I wanted to quit.

"Gary, all through life there're going to be situations that are tough, but to get anywhere you've got to hang in there." My father and twenty-five-year-old cousin, a man who had missed his last year of high school football with a broken leg, were giving me a pep talk that has to challenge Knute Rockne's greatest. "Shoot, it's real easy to quit, anybody can do that, but you don't want to be a quitter. If you quit now it'll just be easier for you to quit again somewhere down along the road. And you don't want to hang your head and run scared." As they spoke they were solemn, leaning forward in their chairs, and the only other thing I remember being conscious of was the soft breeze that blew in my face from an open window.

"Those other boys are no bigger than you. But if you

stand toward the back nobody is going to notice you. You have to get in there and make yourself heard. Why do you think Red plays? [Red was a freckle-faced kid who was smaller than me and was a starter.] Red isn't afraid to get in there and get after it. He makes himself heard. He figures he's just as good as anybody else. Is there any doubt that Red wants to play?"

Again I shook my head no.

"Now when Coach Murphy asks for a volunteer—be first in line—act like you can't wait to get after it—always run—get in there first. You've got to be aggressive, that's what they're looking for. And if you really put everything you've got into it, there's no doubt in our minds that you'll be a starter."

As I looked up at their steady gaze, I felt important. And the pep talk had its effect. In less than two weeks I was starting for the Shetland Ponies. I had beaten Red out of his linebacking position, and by that spring I had become so fanatical that I would lap the rest of the team.

Five years later, playing in my first college football game for the University of Texas, I received another pep talk. We were in Waco to play the Baylor Cubs in the opening freshman game of the season. I was starting left guard and defensive tackle. Pat Culpepper, in his first year as a coach after an All-American season as a player the year before, was giving us a fiery pre-game speech. Suddenly he seemed to lose control and began to rave. I was jerked back as he began beating on the blackboard in a frenzy, tears rolling down his cheeks, and then I was scared. "You're wearing the orange and white—go get 'em; Go get 'em! Go get 'em! Get out there, men!"

I found out later that he always got like that when he was playing, but at the time I felt that it was at least fifty-fifty that I'd gone bananas and was seeing and hearing things. Some of my teammates began pushing and shoving me in a frantic effort to get to the field; and I wasn't sure if they were anxious to get into action, or trying to escape Culpepper. Running through the concrete passageway, many were crying and screaming, a couple of them hitting me on the shoulders saying, "Kill them, Shaw, kill 'em." I had the feeling that I sometimes had when I was a kid and first waking from a nightmare.

As the first team lined up to run pre-game offensive plays, our center, Doug Owens, was almost hysterical. In fact, he had gotten so emotional that on the second play of the game he centered the ball straight up in the air and over the quarterback's head. Leonard Lawrence, the tackle next to me who was from a tiny Texas town, kept waving his arms and yelling, "Aren't you fired up? Aren't you fired up?"—his face a scant six inches from mine. As we lined up for the kickoff I would have given anything to be somewhere else.

At one-hundred-thirty pounds I still didn't like workouts or the hitting, but I tried to stay psyched. Any lapse would result in an immediately playing of the tape about winners and losers that was now in my head. By the ninth grade, I was frequently hearing about the great expectations I had aroused in Denton's senior high coaches.

"Gary, you can get a football scholarship if you want one. I have told only a few other boys this in my eight years of coaching. But you have the potential to play for any college team in the country. It's up to you, and it all depends on what you have inside."

These words were delivered to me solidly and officially, though barely above a whisper, by my high school coach, James Magill. They came right after I had broken an arm in the early part of my junior year. Although I had played in only two games on the high school varsity, neither of them exceptional, I was a "potential star." And from this point until the end of my senior season, I felt I *had* to get a scholarship.

The team doctor had told me that my injury finished me for the year, but my only thought was to make up for my "poor" performance and reward Coach Magill's confidence in me. I was so determined to play that I immobilized my arm in heavy wrapping just for the chance to get into the final two games, and even then, I had to plead to be allowed to play. Though I had only one usable arm, I was fanatical and played better than I ever had. In fact, in just these two games I did well enough to make All-District. This just added to the psyche job I had started on myself for an all-out effort my senior year.

That spring my parents told me that if I wanted to go away to college it would have to be on a scholarship. The coming season would be a real test of my worth.

The summer before my senior year I worked out hard and reported to fall practice in great shape. On the third day of two-a-days we elected co-captains. That afternoon the coaches called me into their office. It was a typical high school field office. Five or six clipboards, play sheets, and schedules were strewn all over the one desk. Pictures of the previous two years' teams and a few faded shots of individual stars in Denton's past covered another. As a sophomore, my distant goal had been to see my individual picture up on the wall. In the corner were weight scales, which seemed to force everyone in to the middle of the tiny room. There were six coaches and only four chairs. When I walked in I was immediately uncomfortable. The faces were neatly squared blocks brought to life only by intense, "responsible" eyes, and I remember my mind juggling the last few days trying to recall if I had done anything that could have brought the anticipated cross-examination. No one spoke, and there was a pause that seemed longer and more serious than any words that could follow.

"Gary, you have been elected a co-captain by the unanimous vote of your teammates. I hope you appreciate this vote of confidence that they have given you. This is an honor, but also a tremendous responsibility. Wherever you are, you must remember that you represent the Bronco football team. This is just as important off the field as on. Your teammates will look to you for an example, and we, the coaches, will be banking on you. To be successful we must have good leadership; you must be completely dedicated."

I left the office thrilled and at the same time feeling tremendously obligated to some vaguely known responsibility.

As a team we were small and slow, not a good combination for winning games. We finished 1-9. After each game in the early part of the season I thought I had done well until film time. Most of the coaches' criticism was directed toward me. On the Monday before the fourth game they moved me from linebacker to lineman, telling me that I wasn't doing the job as linebacker. I was devastated and that afternoon could barely force myself onto the practice field. I felt I had been caught not playing up to my abilities and wanted to apologize to those I had let down. I even began having muscle spasms in my legs whenever I thought of playing our next game, but kept telling myself that I was not a quitter, I would come back. Then on the day of the game, the coaches told me that they would give me one more chance at linebacker. I thought, "This is it."

Before going onto the field, I threw up twice, but by kickoff time I was totally psyched.

After this game and until the last couple of games in the season, I received no comments from the coaches one way or the other. And it was only after the season that I realized that they had manipulated me to get a better performance and had never really considered moving me. I discovered this when I saw the scouting reports of our fourth opponents and saw that their offense had been completely geared toward avoiding me—this after I had supposedly done so horribly my first three games. I was the only player with much ability on the team, and they wanted as much from me as possible. Yet at the time I wasn't even angry at being deceived, because I thought that they must have done it to help me get a scholarship.

My most fanatical game was saved for last. At the time I thought my chances for a scholarship were slim, and I was feeling desperate. As we were getting ready to go on the field, Coach Magill said, "I need a good film on you to show the college coaches—this had better be it."

The next morning he called my father into his office for a private showing of the film. I'd made twenty-five tackles and played my best game. My father was ecstatic.

I still feared not getting a single offer, and I began trying to think of what else I could do. I'd already written to several colleges before our season began, but now I planned to send more letters. "I'll tell them how badly I want to play college football."

But before I could send my second group of letters, an article appeared in the Denton paper's sports page.

Denton High's Gary Shaw learned a valuable lesson the other day—college coaches don't give scholarships for what a boy writes about himself but what he does on the playing field.

Gary, a 196-pound tackle for the Broncos, wrote several letters this past summer to various colleges saying he was interested in playing college football.

T.C.U.'s Walter Roach visited Denton Coach James Magill last week to inquire about the letter and also to talk to a boy he had seen on film.

Magill told Roach, the Frogs' varsity backfield coach, that he thought Shaw was definitely a college prospect.

But evidently Roach wasn't too impressed for he changed the subject and began asking about a No. 74 he had seen game films on. He didn't know the boy's name but had seen enough to know the Frogs were interested.

As luck would have it Shaw and No. 74 were the same person. Roach had a talk with Gary and invited him up to visit the T.C.U. campus sometime this spring.

But it wasn't the letter which had focused the attention of T.C.U. on Shaw, but his performance as an unidentified athlete.

Almost immediately after my last game I had been contacted by several colleges. I was overwhelmed. Within weeks I was getting daily visits from coaches. And I'd love to hear the whispers of "another university to see Shaw" whenever my name was called over the school public address. I was interviewed and written up in the school newspaper listing my offers (about fifteen), and every time I talked to anyone at school they would ask me if I had decided which offer I was taking. Suddenly, I had become a school celebrity.

My first recruiting visit was to Southern Methodist University. After a quick tour of the athletic facilities, I was ushered into head coach Hayden Fry's office. Fry and I

were left alone. I was scared. From behind a square, rigid
oak desk that seemed impenetrable, he stared straight into
my eyes. "I want to know one thing," he said. "Are you a
winner? Are you ready to play for the Southwest Conference Champions in two years?" Relying on what my high
school coach had told me about being confident and direct,
I responded, "Yes, sir."

It seemed so strange that I should even be there with
pictures of all those football greats from Doak Walker to
Don Meredith surrounding me. Also, I had completely
forgotten about my own size, six feet and 196 pounds, and
was awed by all the other visiting "beef." I kept trying to
convince myself that they were scared too, but I really
believed they were unafraid, didn't bruise or bleed, and
were sure of starting in two years. Looking back, I see
seventeen- and eighteen-year-old kids standing in the
S.M.U. coliseum nervously boasting about this game and
that game, each trying to appear as tough and invulnerable
as possible.

But the recruiting incident that made the biggest impression on me happened at the "Harvard of the Southwest," Rice University. Rice has ivy-covered walls and
likes to think of itself as Ivy League, but they tried too
hard to impress me. This feeling extended to football
where Jess Neely, known as the "Southern Gentleman,"
was head coach. As a result, the football players, as well as
the rest of the campus, were unusually tense.

Two second-year men were assigned to show me around.
The first thirty minutes were spent in their discussing all
the places to get a "piece of ass." However, when I made
no comments (I was thinking, "Oh, my God!"), they
nervously changed the subject and decided that we would
go get a couple of six-packs. At the time, I firmly believed

that dedicated football men didn't drink, so while I was downing my Coke, all of us were growing increasingly edgy. Then they must have decided they'd better escalate. "Maybe a strip joint will impress him." Well, Denton didn't have any strip joints, at least that I knew about, and matters grew decidedly worse. Driving back to campus there were two uncomfortable nineteen-year-olds and one very uncomfortable seventeen-year-old. And this incident was the main reason I decided against going to Rice.

When I declined their scholarship offer, Neely was suspicious of my noncommittal response and did some investigating. This included contacting my high school coach, who knew the reasons for my decision. Two days after coming back to Denton my father got a phone call from Neely. He was mad, and in a very indignant manner, he said, "What is this I hear about my boys taking your son drinking? We here at Rice follow the highest principles and don't appreciate false rumors about us. Now I have the two young gentlemen who took your son out standing right here in the office with me. I think they are fine men and they have denied any such action, but if this is true, I will immediately dismiss them from the team and revoke their scholarships. I am waiting for your son's answer." My father turned to me for a response. I told him to lie.

I remember then for the first time being aware of how much power someone like Coach Neely had, and that I had better not do anything wrong in a coach's eyes.

With each new school I visited I felt increasing pressure and tension. Yet everyone around me seemed thrilled. My parents were most excited; they had produced a college football player. Nearly all their friends were avid sports fans, and they, too, had a special interest in my future.

The only person who even considered the possibility that

I might not want to go to college on a football scholarship
was my best friend, Dee Wilson. He was going into his
sophomore year at a small liberal arts school in Colorado.
He had said, "Come up here, the teachers are good, the
weather is great, and there's plenty to do." I allowed myself
to be tempted—but briefly.

My parents tried to remain impartial, but it was obvious
where they wanted me to go. My mother liked the military
academies and Rice. My father liked Texas first and Rice
second, though he never specifically said so. Only one place
they forbade me to visit—the University of Colorado, which
they thought was too wild and had too many beatniks.

As more schools began contacting me, my coach had
man-to-man talks with me. "Gary, I told them that you're
a hitter. I know you won't let me down."

I visited the University of Texas last. Jim Pittman, the
late head coach of T.C.U., recruited me. On his first visit
to Denton, he took my father and me out to dinner. Most
of the conversation was between the two of them. My
father was ready to sign after thirty minutes. Pittman told
him that because of my age—I was to be a seventeen-year-
old freshman—I would be "red-shirted." He said that the
marvelous thing about this was that it gave me an extra
free year of schooling. He gave me the usual bit about
being able to see me in orange and white (Texas colors),
and that he had never missed on a boy yet. The only comment he made directly to me was, "Gary, we like to hit at
Texas and I know you're a hitter."

Finally one weekend I visited the Texas campus, with
about thirty other prospects. On Saturday afternoon we all
met in the letterman's lounge at the top of Texas' Memorial
Stadium. The lounge was filled with beautiful coeds, in-

cluding the University Sweetheart—and they were there to talk us into coming to Texas. Surrounding these girls were trophies and pictures of Texas greats, color television, a long bar, and a beautiful orange rug. I was excited and laughing nervously. I felt that I was as important as anyone my age could possibly be. Every prospect had three coeds surrounding him, and like me, stood goggle-eyed and speechless as they told us how much they wanted us to come to Texas. If you are seventeen and there are three or four beautiful twenty-one-year-old women standing around you, telling you to do something, you are apt to do it. But the real reason I decided to go to Texas was the fact that my girlfriend, a high school junior, was thinking of coming to Texas a year hence.

My parents had also come to Austin and we were all staying at the Villa Capri Motel. We were eating in the motel restaurant when I saw Coach Royal for the first time. He had a disarming smile and wore a bright Texas-orange sweater. His easiness and poise was in direct contrast to the tension that gripped my mother, father, and me. He was distant, yet at the same time seemed happy to see us. "I hope [looking at my parents] you are enjoying yourselves— glad you could come down." I felt the immediate urge to assure him that they were. Then, "I'm looking forward to having Gary come down and play some football for us. He's a fine football player," and he turned and smiled at me. He then suggested some places my parents might enjoy visiting and asked if there was anything he could do for us. He gave us the feeling that what he was doing was a favor, but a favor done graciously. The rest of the conversation was brief, and when he left, my mother's first comment was about his charm. He had seemed to feel de-

cidedly superior, yet paradoxically he had managed to con-
vey a manner empty of arrogance. I hoped that I had made
a good impression on him.

On February 12, I signed with Texas. Jim Pittman came
up to sign me and the next day my picture and the story
covered the Denton sports page. I was just glad it was over
—the pressure was off and I would not have to worry about
it for six months. With school friends this was true as
things gradually settled back to normal. However, with
adults I still found it impossible to escape the topic. "Will
Royal play you at linebacker?" "When are you going to
Texas? I know you'll be starting in two years." "Will Texas
win the conference next year?" "What do you think of
Royal?" As far as they were concerned I had no other
identity, and gradually I came to have the strange feeling
that I was an imposter, a hoax. I had not even gone to
Texas yet and here I was already a big star. I remember
the horrible thought that ran through my mind more than
once: What if I'm too scared to even go out on the practice
field?

Arriving at Texas

In late August of 1963, 44 of us freshmen were unloaded in the southeast corner of the Texas campus. We were delivered by family cars, rented trailers, and beaming mamas and papas. Our nervous intrusion onto the otherwise deserted campus was witnessed only by the omnipresent Texas tower. The tower juts up hundreds of feet from the heart of that sprawling academic complex, and life at Texas orbits around its thirty stories. It's both the symbol of student-body pride and Texas football prowess. After every gridiron victory its top is lighted bright orange and it can be seen from almost any point in Austin.

We arrived two weeks before the rest of the student body and, at best, we felt insignificant as we crowded onto the hot sidewalk outside Moore-Hill Hall, the athletic dormitory. The rest of the campus seemed distant and foreboding, and the isolation of the athletic compound was comforting. Our arrival was mainly an occasion for parents. Unmistakably proud, they seemed to bask in the warmth of the thought they had produced a Texas Longhorn. They mingled readily, exchanging hearty greetings. Their manner exuded confidence that their offspring was a prize acquisition. In contrast, we "future stars" milled about the perimeter obviously nervous and most interested in putting up a steady front.

Two families would meet, the parents would exchange a warm greeting with easy laughter; the players would shake hands and nod. The parents would discuss the coming Longhorn season and their respective progeny. The players' remarks were limited to "Where did you play high school

16

ball?" and "What is your position?" All our words and actions seemed directed toward presenting a tough image. A subtle playacting to this end was used from the very first day, and would continue throughout our careers.

When I met a future teammate that first day my body tensed and a little psychological game began. My voice got tougher, and if no adults were around, my language got a little cruder. I felt the need to get across how blasé I was about the whole thing—just another day. I quickly learned the art of innocent comments to let my future "enemy" know that I was ready for him, like "Do you know when we are going to put on the pads?" said in a way to convince him that I was eager for action.

Any fears had to be carefully cloaked, especially the fear of hitting. These fears crept out very indirectly if at all. It was only occasionally that we shared them in a small bit of silent camaraderie. For example, that first day there were three or four of us, all linemen, standing together in the hall when a quarterback by the name of Tommy Cade walked by. Cade had weightlifter's shoulders and huge legs, and outweighed the tackle next to me, Wayne Suttle, by twenty pounds. As this mass of bricked muscles passed us, we all knew that we'd have to tackle this hulk in the near future. After Cade had passed out of hearing range, Suttle said, "That's a big son-of-a-bitch for a quarterback." The rest of us knew what he meant.

Many of the arriving players wore cowboy hats and boots, making some of them seem giants as they stretched into the Texas sun. One of the first I saw was Rusty Workman, who was to be my roommate the first two years. He was wearing orange (Texas orange) colored boots and in these boots he stood a good six foot three or four and weighed 215 to 220 pounds. He was a "Blue Chip" player from Arlington. Blue Chip players are boys selected by the coaches as "Can't miss," best in the state. He had huge shoulders, a hooked nose, and he didn't smile. I remember my mother saying, "Boy, he looks mean."

As we anxiously milled around that first day getting acquainted, we would have been shocked to see into the near future, shocked at how many of us would be going home to disappointed parents before a single year had gone by. Only a year from this day several of us would be sitting on the steps of Moore-Hill musing over the tenseness of the incoming freshmen and laughing at their parents' beaming faces. While these new recruits were unpacking, we would be placing bets on how many of them would be left come June. However, as I walked into the dorm on this first day, these events were part of an unknown future. Pat Culpepper was sitting at a desk passing out room cards. He was one of the freshman coaches. As I went in, he introduced himself, told me my room number, and had me sign one of the cards. Then he informed me when and where supper would be served. After my parents helped me move my luggage into my room, I walked them to the car. My stomach had never been more empty. My father said, "Give 'em all you've got." My mother cried, and when I got back to my room, so did I.

Just before supper the first night, we were ordered to the side door of the dining room by the varsity who were in the midst of fall two-a-day workouts. For ten minutes the doors were kept locked as the varsity were seated. Then finally an anonymous voice said, "You can come in now," and the doors opened. Suddenly a low-pitched growl burst on us. We were in the midst of one hundred disembodied voices gone mad. We jumped back and hugged the walls while this jeering and growling kept steady for about five

minutes. It was our first taste of one of the principles of football: intimidation. We all just stood in the doorway, not
sure whether to smile to indicate that we were good sports
or whether to remain grim to let them know we took it
seriously. It was much easier to look serious.

"Sit down, freshmen!" Just as my bottom touched the
seat: "Stand up freshmen! Who told you to sit down?"
Everyone jumped up but one paralyzed frosh three chairs
down. Immediately he was told to come to the top steps of
the dining room. The rest of us were rather pointedly asked
why we were still standing. This sit-and-stand continued
while the single freshman standing at the front was told
one thing to do by one and the opposite by another. He
then sang a medley of songs, everything from "Eyes of
Texas" to "All I Want for Christmas Is My Two Front
Teeth." Before supper was over, twenty to thirty of us had
been called out for these individual performances. I just
tried to follow orders and look as inconspicuous as possible.

This kind of scene was to go on until the end of the first
semester. We usually ended up eating about half of each
meal on our feet. For the most part the dining room was
controlled bedlam. This atmosphere had immediate effects
besides indigestion. We got as much food as we wanted,
but by the third day we had learned to be quick with our
hands in order to get any meat. Each evening over a hundred football jocks stood with heads bowed behind their
chairs, forks in hand ready to stab for the meat plate as
soon as the dinner prayer was over.

At first I was flabbergasted. Three different servings of
meat would be gone before I'd had my first bite. The usual
practice was to stack food high on your plate—always more
than any two could handle. If anyone said he didn't want

his dessert, the nearest players went after it with forks. This was one race big linemen usually won. In short, you ate aggressively. People would take "pass this or that" literally. Bread flew across the table with regularity. It was almost as if you had to show how voracious you could be—as if this was some verification of virility. I quickly found myself caught up in it. I ate fast, with mouth open, and more than once I responded to a gruff "pass the potatoes" by tossing them—bowl and all.

It was after supper that the real hazing began. This ranged from shining shoes (some of the bigger-named freshmen would have to shine fifteen to twenty pairs a night), to favorite games. One of the favorite games was "Cuckoo."

Cuckoo took two freshmen to play. In my first game, my partner was Bill Sullivan, a big end from Houston. We were taken to a varsity player's room. No other freshmen were allowed in. We were surrounded by second- and third-year men. After some "teasing" to warm up—"Well, men, we got some fresh meat here, some real high school stars." They blindfolded us. They then told me to get on top of one of the desks, and told Sullivan to get underneath it. Then, handing me a rolled up Sunday newspaper, a churlish second-year tackle said, "Freshman, do you know what this is?"

I nodded my head yes.

"Freshman, I want you to take this and knock the shit out of Sullivan when we tell you to." He then swatted me over the head and said, "Like that—got the picture?"

I was to hit Sullivan, swinging as hard and fast as possible whenever I heard the word "cuckoo." Sullivan was, on command, to make himself an available target by sticking his head out from under the desk. When his head was clear of the desk, he let me know by saying "cuckoo." In fact, he had to leave his head exposed until they told him he could pull it back. As long as his head was outside the desk, I was to be swinging from above my head with both hands.

"Shaw, if you don't start hitting him harder than that you're going to be spending a lot of time under that desk. Man, that's pathetic. Get up, Sullivan. Shaw, get your ass down under there if you're not going to hit any harder than a pussy."

I hadn't been hitting Sullivan as hard as I could because I still half thought they were kidding.

But when I got under the desk Sullivan proceeded to smash me. He took them at their word. They loved it. "Now that's it, Sullivan. Shaw, get your head back out there." (I kept jerking my head back in because it was surprisingly painful—though each time I did, my time under the desk would be extended.)

Finally, more out of fear than pain, I left it exposed until all the varsity men in the room were satiated. Many minutes afterward I was still dizzy, but more than being physically upset, I was frightened. I was frightened at how hard it had been for me to really hit Sullivan compared with how easy it had seemed for him. I felt timid, unaggressive, and out of place.

Probably the varsity's most popular game was "Record Races." Here they would strip several of us naked and divide us into two groups. Then, they would bring out our "toy"—an old 45-rpm record. They placed the toy between the cracks of our asses. We had to carry it from one end of the hall to the other without using our hands. We would then have to—again without using our hands—place it in our teammate's ass. If he happened to drop it, his partner had to pick it up with his mouth, and put it back in place. These races were considered the highlight of the evening.

Like everyone else, I developed all kinds of stratagems to avoid as much of this as possible. When I left the dining hall I'd try to leave in a crowd. To leave too early or too late was disastrous. The varsity lined up in the main halls outside the dining room to await us, so I'd try to sneak out the side door and around the building and up the side staircase. It was remarkable how many other freshmen I ran into. The most important thing was to remain as inconspicuous as possible. If you ever lost your cool and let it show, like talking back, you were a marked man. The most restraint had to be used when a varsity player called at one or two in the morning telling you to run and get him a Coke.

Though we had to prove that we were "good sports," it was still wise to get across the point that we weren't real wild about the games. We walked a narrow tightrope, but to avoid becoming complete guinea pigs, we had to plant the seed of possibility that we would "whip some ass" on the field come spring training. All these games were supposedly done in good fun and on the premise that they helped build team morale. The coaches, without saying so specifically, endorsed them and told the varsity not to get too carried away. And these "morale builders" did have the one good effect of keeping our freshman minds on specifics—like avoiding the varsity each day. Yet behind the guffaws and grins, these games were conducted in earnest.

One purpose of this hazing, as I've already mentioned, was intimidation. We threatened the already insecure world of second- and third-year players, especially redshirts. These players were the most likely casualties of our battlefield competition.

But more importantly, hazing initiated us into a world of unquestioning obedience. On command we needed to be able to demonstrate the required amount of self-denial. Because if we willingly put ourselves through what older players had gone through, then they had some "reassurance" for the worth of their own self-abuse. The next year we would try to exact this same reassurance from new freshmen.

This hazing compounded our bewilderment and confusion. We were eighteen-year-old high school heroes lost in a new world and daily being stripped of dignity and any past identity. The more glorious our past, the more important it became for the varsity to impress on us that our past meant nothing now. Increasingly for all of us, there was only one place to look for authority and direction—the coaches and "Daddy D."

Daddy D was Coach Royal. The D stood for Darrell and was the name we players used in referring to him among ourselves. This name, as well as his manner in the initial week of confusion, gave me my first hint of the impersonal father-son relationship that would exist between us.

At supper our second night Daddy D spoke his first words to us. He told us that we had a lot of work ahead and carefully outlined the next couple of days. He was to the point and businesslike. This was to be his general tone throughout my four years at Texas. Somehow even this brevity of speech added to my feelings of a shrinking world. He said that we were there to do an important job —prepare ourselves to help the University of Texas win

football games. Royal was very serious. He wanted us to
start getting it into our skulls right then that all else was
irrelevant.

I wanted to get away, to retreat to some small restaurant
in Denton with my high school girlfriend, Gail. Just sit
over in the corner and hold hands. I had a big picture of
her on my desk, and when I looked at her it was with
the feeling that this new world was some crazy dream and
would somehow soon evaporate. At first I willfully tried
to keep my mind on her, my parents, my high school, and
Denton as if concentration would magically dissolve everything around me. Fear, however, moved in on this fading
past, and I began to worry that everyone would soon discover
that I was out of place and see me as weak. Once discovered,
I would be chiselled until I broke. So I determined to avoid
any more of these thoughts about home and the past.

However, I still couldn't escape some pernicious dread,
and so I fell back on an old habit, long walks. My nightly
strolls took me through the capital grounds of Austin and
over every foot of Texas's expansive campus. Under the
peaceful and open skies I felt lonely and out of kilter. Yet,
as I strolled the streets, I would gradually come to feel a
natural part of the night's calm. This seemed so different
from the tension inside Moore-Hill Hall. The longer I
walked, the more bizarre and unreal Moore-Hill seemed.
Sometimes I could even feel myself loosen up, sigh, almost
go limp . . . but immediately I would reprimand myself.
I couldn't relax and let go. I had to be mentally prepared
—we were to put on pads in five days.

We spent the first several days' workouts in shorts. On
defense I was a linebacker; there were fifteen of us. On
offense I was a left guard; seven of us. The day before we
put on pads, I was running second team behind Jim Haley,

the fastest lineman on the team. These ratings were based on agility, hustle, and previous reputation, but everybody knew they didn't count until the hitting started. The most interesting thing about these workouts was how body-conscious and weight-conscious everyone was. We were all in shorts and T-shirts, and I found myself constantly checking out other bodies and noticing other players doing the same. I concentrated on legs and forearms. Big forearms worried me most. I could easily envision them cracking the side of my face. I knew so well what one in full force did when it connected with my nose. Guys with extraordinary legs usually got the most comments: "Look at that son-of-a-bitch's legs," followed by a nervous laugh. The size of the calf seemed directly proportional to power. Strangely, though, the guys who were smaller than most also aroused fear, a kind of uneasy apprehension that they must really be mean to be that small and still have been awarded a scholarship to Texas. All through the week in shorts the coaches, especially Culpepper, kept reminding us that in a few days we'd all find out who the "real men" were.

Traditionally at Texas, the first day in pads is to be a scrimmage against the varsity. The older players, mostly surviving second-year men, had told us all week that we were going to get hit like we'd never been hit before. While working out in shorts the locker room had been noisy and rowdy. The first day in pads there was silence. I hadn't hit anyone in ten months and I was getting ready to go against the team that was to win the national championship that year. Many of the big-name players were people I'd read about. Now I was going up against them. The anticipation of this unknown was like nothing else I've ever experienced.

All athletes have moments of anxious anticipation. Every time you try out for a new team there is apprehension, but this was more. I was going to be slamming into men two to four years older, some who outweighed me twenty to forty pounds, and the last time I'd hit was at Denton against boys I usually outweighed by fifteen pounds. What was the difference going to be like? How bad would it hurt? What would it feel like? I kept telling myself that in three hours it would all be over with.

The bathroom seemed to be the single area of full movement and perhaps our only way of sharing mutual fear. I pissed about five times just in the process of getting my uniform on. As was always the case with me, the real symbolic act was putting on my helmet. It is an act of loneliness—shutting the world off completely from the thoughts and fears running through by head. My face was mostly hidden and the thing that became important was the color of my jersey and its number. I always had the feeling that when I pulled my helmet on, it was each man for himself, and each had his own private battles. But the helmet usually felt protective because it was familiar and gave me the feeling that only so much damage could be done. Yet this day it seemed extremely heavy and somehow very breakable.

If you watch closely you'll notice that in any locker room most players perform their individual rituals immediately before they go onto the field. For me, it was one last look in the locker to make sure my clothes and personal possessions were in place. I guess there was some kind of security in the idea that they would be arranged the same way when I came back again—an element of permanence that I could count on.

When we got on the field the varsity was still watching

films. So the coaches called us together and said, "All right,
we're going to start finding out who likes to hit." The guards
and tackles then went over to one section of the field, the
backs to another.

The first contact came as a welcome relief. In fact the
pain of impact was barely noticed. The torture was that
we graded each other closely; I felt so exposed.

One instance that first day stands out as vividly as any
other in my four years at Texas. The coaches were pairing
studs against studs and the two they were most excited
about seeing were two high school "Blue Chip" All-American ends. They were Bill Sullivan from Houston and Kelly
Baker from Dumas. Baker stood six foot seven and weighed
230 pounds. Sullivan was six two and 215. Baker's laurels
had mostly come from pass receiving. When they put these
two on the boards the whole team was watching. One
coach's comment was: "Now we'll see what stuff these two
All-Americans have got." Two gladiators on display. Both
were tense, and Sullivan jumped the count twice, smashing
Baker's head both times. They went three times, and Sullivan wiped out Baker all three times. The coaches were
hovering over Baker and yelling at him to put some of that
All-American beef behind him—and couldn't seem to tell
him enough how badly Sullivan was "whipping his ass."
Baker was humiliated. He pretended not to notice that
everyone was watching. For several days this confrontation
was a topic of conversation with the rest of us, and for a
long time Baker had the reputation of not liking to hit.
It was the worst and most difficult stigma one could carry.
Sullivan quit football after his sophomore year—Baker
was one of a handful that was around the full four years,
and ended up starting at end his last year. But he never
rose above third team end on the freshman squad, and

I always wondered how long it took him to get over that first day.

After this drill I went to linebacking drills—Pat Culpepper was in charge of these. For five straight days all the linebackers did was head-on tackling. At the end of the first day there were a couple of broken bones, a broken nose, and a brain concussion just from Culpepper's drills.

By the time the varsity finally came onto the field, our coaches had decided to wait a couple of days before scrimmaging them. As always in these situations, several freshmen acted disappointed, as if they really wanted at them. I gues they really thought that the coaches might believe them. I didn't.

At the start of the second day, I was still second team. By the third day, I was starting. I was defeating Jim Haley, my main competition, in our one-on-one warfare. I was starting left guard, which meant I also started at defensive tackle. The whole first week was hit, hit, then again—especially the linebackers. Everytime I would look around it seemed someone was down and Culpepper was repeating one of his favorite sayings, "If you're putting out you don't get hurt." I had fortunately been moved to defensive tackle the second day, but even at my position the whole first week was a daze. My mind was empty and all I was really conscious of was how physically tired I was, that my body ached, and that I had to have a good workout that afternoon to stay ahead of Haley. But when this constant contact stopped, things had been completely rearranged.

I wasn't reacted to as the same person. All freshmen who now passed me in the hall called me by my first name. It was the difference between going into Nieman-Marcus with dirty bluejeans, unshaven face and T-shirt, and then going in wearing an expensive business suit. From those who hadn't made the first team, I was easily granted superiority, and a little fear was never too far below the surface. It was the same with the rest of the starters. To be a starter said much more to everyone than just football ability.

The players in the worst position were those who had tried to come on strong before the hitting began, and then didn't do well once it started. For example, I had developed a special dislike for one freshman because of his outward arrogance and condescension toward others. His name was Johnny G——. There were a few others that I also had this special hostility to, and this kind of dislike usually had a strong element of fear. Johnny had been at several of the schools I'd visited the past spring, and he had always talked about how he could hardly wait to get at it—he "would ring some bells." He really came on as the big, mean stud. I'd even thought about him during the summer, what kind of forearm I'd give him when we had our first contact. Then he'd regret playing the big stud with me.

What a shock it was when I realized Johnny was scared, and he didn't want to hit at all . . . and he wouldn't. Within a week he'd become the nice guy on the field, trying to placate me and others. He was on the last team all fall and gone within a few months. Culpepper always used to get him to carry the ball (he was a lineman) during tackling drills because that's what he hated most. Gradually, Johnny almost seemed to become even apologetic when speaking to me and others around the dorm—as if he'd been found out, and would we forgive him. I remember thinking what a phony chickenshit he was. But gradually this feeling turned to something else as he came to be treated as an untouchable by the rest. And when he left I don't remember anyone even noticing or mentioning it.

There were some who seemed to have total dedication to being a football player for Texas. One was Rusty, my roommate. He was a starter from the first day. By the third day, Culpepper was holding him up as an example to the others. On the fifth day, in a linebacker tackling drill, he was hit by a seventh team fullback, Charles Owens. As far as the Texas coaches were concerned, his Blue-chip value as a player was over. It was his knee. Usually when a knee goes you can hear it snap, as if you'd popped a big wishbone in two. But this was much louder than usual. It sounded more like the cracking of shoulder pads slamming together. Rusty immediately screamed and then started rolling around on the ground, moaning. Culpepper's first reaction was to start yelling at Owens, whom he didn't like. "Owens, get up! Get up! Get off the ground, you sorry . . ." He didn't curse because he thought it immoral. "Owens, it should be you down there instead of Workman."

I was stunned and wanted to turn my head from the whole scene. Rusty never really recovered from this injury and just two years later I heard Coach Mike Campbell, the head defensive coach, call him gutless and order him to get off the field.

Little did I realize that what I saw and felt these first few days was a picnic compared to what was to follow.

Rusty

In the spring of 1963, Darrell Royal said to a reporter, "Rusty Workman is the kind of football player we want. He didn't ask me what his chances were of making the team, or how many other fullbacks there were, just that he wanted to play for Texas."

I've never known anyone any more gung-ho football and Texas than Russell (Rusty) Workman. He was a fullback and linebacker for Arlington High School when I met him for the first time on the playing field. Our Denton High scouting report had Rusty as being the best fullback and linebacker we'd face, and he was. As a linebacker he completely pulverized our right offensive guard. This guard had a reputation of being very tough, and yet by half time he was feigning illness to have an excuse for his poor play during the second half. Rusty really punished him, and by the fourth quarter this guard's helmet was heading straight for the ground on every snap. Rusty also ran over us at fullback, and at one point met our middle linebacker head-on, and drove him straight back five yards on his way to the end zone.

Rusty's face was a cross between a boxer and one of the heavies in a Roman gladiator movie. He had a hooked Roman nose, and his lips curled downward in a scowl. I could never find an innocent spot on his face, and it was hard to believe he was only eighteen. He was an awesome figure when walking down the hall with his big Texas orange-colored boots that he always wore.

When I first saw Rusty I thought he was one of the ugliest guys I'd ever seen. His girlfriend, Margaret, now his wife, was one of the prettiest girls I'd ever seen. In the athletic dorm at Texas there were several players who had a crush on Margaret, but even when they mentioned her name it was in a whisper. I don't think any of them would have gone out with her if she had called and begged.

Rusty told me our first week at Texas, "There are only two things that matter to me—that's playing football at Texas and Margaret." Dogged perseverance shone through Rusty's face and was announced in his every step.

"Gary, I'm going to start at Texas as a sophomore."

In many ways Rusty seemed to be what we all felt we were supposed to be; what fathers want from their sons and coaches from their players. He believed all the right things—"If you want it you can get it!"—that the world was rationally structured with the good guys always coming out on top. That didn't mean things might not get tough before you won, but he had the firm conviction he was a "fourth quarter" man. Indeed, Rusty had as much physical courage and toughness as anyone I've ever known. One of his best friends once said of him: "Rusty is completely straightforward and honest. There is not a pretentious bone in his body. And when he goes after something it is with total dedication."

These first years at Texas all Rusty's dedication was channeled into football. He never broke training and had no respect for those that did. In the ninth grade I used to carry notebook paper around and mark in hours and minutes how long it was to the next Rice football game. That was Rusty at Texas.

He firmly believed dedication should be transmitted through action not words. "You should let your shoulder pads do the talking." Rusty would frequently not say anything—even in a crowd. Finally one of us asked him why he didn't talk more. Rusty simply said, " 'Cause I haven't got anything to say."

Rusty was quite intelligent. But he was eighteen and single-minded; his whole world was football. This single-mindedness made him the most respected player on the freshman team. And Culpepper had his perfect model.

Yet there was another side to Rusty, a playfulness at odds with his religious seriousness about football. An incident that happened late one night during our second year made it impossible for me to ever keep from liking him. Rusty was a Dr. Pepper addict; loved them. During the course of a day, if I were to hear only one statement from him it would most likely be, "Shaw, I'm going to get a Dr. Pepper. Want one?"

One particular night about midnight I heard this high-pitched giggle and then Rusty burst into the room carrying a whole case of Dr. Pepper. He was just mumbling, "Machine broke . . . Dr. Peppers coming out . . . Dr. Pepper machine . . . hurry . . . !"

He jerked me up and started full tilt down the hall, jumping in the air with those big orange boots about every third step. At the end of the hall was a Dr. Pepper machine. Covering the floor beneath it were broken Dr. Pepper bottles with, as Rusty said, "The sweet smell of D. P. everywhere." He had put ten cents in the machine and the bottles kept coming out one after another. He had three or four full cases stacked up against the wall and kept giggling as he rushed up to put in another dime, not even noticing there weren't any cases left. I really thought he was going to throw his arms around this broken-down machine in a lover's embrace. Brigitte Bardot in the nude with thousand-dollar bills stuck to her waist couldn't have meant as much to Rusty as those Dr. Peppers. We had Dr.

Peppers under our bed for weeks, and all Rusty could say was, "They just kept coming and coming."

When Rusty played or laughed, it was with abandon; there was no in-between. But there was also never any doubt about where the bulk of his energy was going. He wanted to be a Texas Longhorn.

After Rusty had torn up his knee in our first week, he was out of action for the rest of that freshman season.

"I could hardly take it. I'd never been injured in high school."

Rusty's injury turned out to be more serious than the doctor had thought, and he also had to miss our first spring training. Yet when he came back for two-a-days in the fall, he still said, "I'm going to play this year." But early in this second fall Rusty pulled ligaments in his ankle and was out for six weeks. He had a good spring training his sophomore year, then the next fall he received his third serious injury. This time it was his leg, and he missed six more crucial weeks. Rusty's final injury came the following spring, our third year. He separated a shoulder. It was this fourth major injury that finished him. His shoulder was so badly separated that if he hit a bump in the road while driving his car, it would pop out of place. As his "playing stock" declined, Rusty was stunned at the treatment he received from the coaches.

Rusty is currently a successful personnel director for a Houston firm and several years from his playing days at Texas, but he remains deeply affected by what happened to him. "Royal put the screw-offs, the injured, and those who lacked 'physical abilities' into one big bracket. You either performed or you didn't. You were either one or the other," he said.

"What do you think of Royal?" I asked him.

"I think he is a master politician and smooth administrator, but I really don't know him."

"Do you think Royal really knew anything about you or the rest of us?"

"Oh, yow, I think Royal really did know his players. He was too smart not to. But I guess he felt that if he were ever to show that he understood one of his players and respond to him with human qualities, then others could manipulate him and make attempts to gain his sympathy. So he didn't respond to anyone that way. He kept his power and there was no way to get to him."

"How many times in your three years did you ever talk with Royal?"

"Three or four times, only once or twice when it didn't pertain to injuries."

"Wasn't it an injury that finally led to your quitting?"

"Yow, Frank [Medina the head trainer] kept telling me it was a bruise [talking about his shoulder], but I could feel it pop every time I moved. I knew it was more than a bruise."

"Wouldn't he let you go see a doctor?"

"No, but I finally went on my own anyway. The doctor said that I had a bad separation, and if I'd come in when it first happened, I'd probably had an operation. But he said that during all the weeks that I'd been playing with it, it had gotten somewhat back together on its own and that now I could probably get by without getting cut on." (Injured players who fell below a certain team often had a problem gaining permission to see the team physician.)

"When did you know it was getting close to the end?"

"Right after I'd gone to the doctor we had a big scrimmage [this was our third spring] and I didn't play. Royal then sent me and a bunch of others down to the end of the field for 'shit drills.' I remember he came over to the side of me after I had just finished carrying the ball and said in a sarcastic tone, 'Workman, if you could keep from getting hurt, you might get to play some around here.' At the end of the shit drills I was so upset I took my helmet and threw it across the field."

"What did Royal say to you when you went in to tell him you were quitting?"

"He said, 'Okay, fine.' "

"Then I told him that I felt I had earned and deserved my scholarship and that I wouldn't be quitting unless I was really hurt. My shoulder was hurting enough that I couldn't even sleep at night.

"Royal said, 'To keep your scholarship it has to be medically approved that you're unable to play.' [1]

"So I went to Dr. Buckley [the team surgeon], and he told me that I could play again if I had an operation, or if I learned a new blocking style."

"A new blocking style?"

"Yow, blocking without using my shoulder! I took these reports back to Royal. Royal said that according to the reports I was medically able to play. But I told him that I was quitting and going to keep my scholarship anyway. He waited for awhile and then said, 'Okay.' "

(Royal backed down quite easily in this case. Could it have been the fact that Rusty's father was the athletic director of the Arlington public schools as well as being an influential former coach?)

"If I hadn't been injured I'd never have quit. One thing I knew I couldn't and wouldn't let them do is run me off— noway, nohow."

---

[1] This is completely inaccurate. See the *Handbook of the Southwest Athletic Conference,* p. 49.

"As it was, how did you feel about quitting?"

"Crushed . . . humiliated. My whole world came tumbling down. I don't know what would have happened to me if Margaret and my father hadn't stood by me. My father treated me as though I were the same person. I felt like I let you guys down. I'd broken the 'code.' "

"What code?"

"The code we had, to agree to never quit, never give in, never give up. I didn't feel like I could face any of you. I thought you would look down on me. Still to this day, Gary, I feel you and the others who stuck it out all the way have something inside of you that I don't have. I still have respect for you because of that reason. I guess I'll really never get over it."

"How long do you think it took to regain your self-confidence after you quit?"

"It took me at least three years to accept the fact that I had quit, and could still do other worthwhile things. And still, when I go back to see old players on the team or old coaches, I feel embarrassed, ashamed."

"Did you get anything positive out of football at Texas?"

"Yeah, I learned that you've got to be flexible."

"What do you mean?"

"You can't put yourself in a position where your whole life is just based on one thing, because if you do, and you don't cut it, you're wiped out. Anytime you've been that dedicated to something for that long, even when you have to give it up, it will always be part of you. I still have fantasies about going back and redeeming myself."

Our Education

Football is not a democracy. There's nothing to debate. The players can debate in political science class.

—Carl De Pasqua, football coach,
University of Pittsburgh

Football bears the same relation to education that bull-fighting does to agriculture.

—Elbert Hubbard

All education today is therapy: therapy in the sense of liberating man by all available means from a society in which, sooner or later, he is going to be transformed into a brute, even if he doesn't notice it anymore.

—Herbert Marcuse

All I know is that when everyone else moves, I move, and when everyone files on the bus, I get on the bus . . . I really don't know what time it is, what day it is . . . I don't know anything at all.

—Jerry Kramer

One of the reasons I had picked Texas was for its academic reputation. Royal had assured me and my folks that one of his main concerns was that all his players get a degree and a good education. My parents and I had been impressed that Royal had hired a "brain coach" whose only job was to help the athletes with their education.

But Lan Hewlett, the Texas brain coach, spoke like a salesman who had long ago forgotten his product. He went through all the right body movements, but behind his horn-rimmed glasses his face was motionless. The ironic thing was that Hewlett believed what he was saying. Tensely bent forward, Hewlett, a gaunt and wizened figure, frequently said of our schooling: "It is like in football. We believe every player plays better when he knows the rules of the game. We simply join the many other services of the university in trying to get the game rules to the participants." [1]

Hewlett met with the freshmen the first couple of days we were at Texas and each time recited his canned exhortations about discipline and education. The more he spoke the more I strained to hear his words. Yet the more I leaned toward him the easier it seemed for his syllables to slip behind me. And even with the belief that what Hewlett said to us was definitely important, I still couldn't keep some flighty disinterest under control. I remember thinking all through college that overcoming this conflict was what was meant by concentration in the classroom— wrinkling my face and forcing back any feeling.

---

[1] Official Longhorn Program, Texas v. Arkansas—Dec. 5, 1970, p. 6.

The setting for these meetings with Hewlett were just like team meetings—we all had spiral notebooks and No. 2 lead pencils that were clenched tightly and ready to put down anything that appeared remotely important. As Hewlett talked I felt that these courses were more obstacles, mental tackling dummies that had to be mowed down.

At the end of these "educational" meetings, I felt and acted just like I did after our team meetings. I'd crowd for the exit, and as soon as I got out I'd playfully shove or goose a teammate. Like everyone else, I was loud and boisterous. This seemed a momentary release, but just like a half-opened carbonated beverage, something inside of me was not able to escape. After our first week with Hewlett, I knew our education, like football, was to be spelled D-I-S-C-I-P-L-I-N-E, and that I needed to start psyching myself to be ever ready.

As an aid to this mechanical preparation, our lives were strictly regimented. Hewlett had arranged our fall classes in the morning and early afternoon. We went from one to another, from desk to desk, until two P.M. Then we prepared for our football workout. For me, it was sometimes hard to tell the difference between my classes and workouts. In both I quickly finished one part, then moved on to the next. The object was to get through them and accomplish my mission, their defeat. And after succeeding, I would move on to another course—another contest.

We were usually at the field house by two-thirty for taping. By three-thirty we were on the field. Workouts lasted until about five-thirty. By the time we showered and got back to the dorm it was time for supper at six. My first semester the freshmen were to be at a required study hall at seven. Study hall was over at ten. Back to the dorm and to bed. Every activity was oriented toward getting us disciplined and well oiled. Success and winning meant denial, doing what was not easy—not liked. Study hall was another such challenge, another test of will. I hated walking to and being in study hall as a group, as if knowledge was something to be defeated and we could do it better as a team. We studied in a room on the third floor of the English building, yet I couldn't help but feel we were still on the field. Every time my mind strayed I felt it to be a lack of character. If I couldn't do it here, I couldn't do it on the field. I remember at first almost being superstitious about screwing off. I thought that if I didn't work hard in study hall, I would be guaranteed a bad workout the next day. So I responded by studying even harder, and at ten I usually left the English building with a headache.

To be sure that we didn't stray from this tight regimen, we were required to turn in class attendance reports each Monday at three P.M. These reports, called cut slips, were dropped in a small locked box outside Hewlett's office. They were to record time and place of any class absence from the previous week. We were not to miss a class for any reason, and Hewlett was responsible for validating the accuracy of our reports. He did so by periodically checking with our professors. If inaccuracies were discovered or absences reported, Hewlett informed Coach Royal. Coach Royal then delegated disciplinary action, and usually those disciplined were to rise at four-thirty in the morning to "run the stands" under the supervision of Frank Medina, the head trainer. To run the stands meant to run to the top steps of Texas's stadium, back down, and then up again, etc., for a minimum of thirty minutes. While running these stands we wore ankle weights, wrist weights, and either a twenty- or thirty-pound weighted vest.

When we joined the varsity, this regimentation and its

seriousness was increased. In fact, very few things were important enough to interfere with Royal's tight organization. For example, the day President Kennedy was shot in Dallas, the varsity was on the practice field preparing for Texas A & M at their regularly scheduled time—two hours after Kennedy's death. Royal told us that this is what President Kennedy would have wanted us to do.

During the season the varsity had workouts Monday through Thursday, which, including the coming and going, took approximately three to four hours. On Fridays, there was a brief workout in sweats and later a pep rally. Right after the rally the coaches took us to the Holiday Inn where we stayed until game time. The purpose of going to a motel was to avoid any pre-game distractions. And, of course, Saturday was the day of the game, leaving Sunday as our one free day.

Even then we were expected to indulge in a little postgame limbering up. As for the nights, besides Friday and Saturday, we had films Mondays and Tuesdays. These came right after supper and usually lasted until nine-thirty or so. Thus, in the time requiring our physical presence we had at least a thirty- to forty-hour work week. Interestingly enough, the university will not let anyone who is working over thirty hours take a full course load (anything over nine hours), yet all of us were taking a bare minimum of ten hours and most of us twelve to fifteen hours.

With our severe lack of study time, Coach Royal explained that he had to apply the same discipline to our classroom attendance as he applied to our football performance. He wanted to make sure that we attended classes because he thought it just as important to be a winner in the classroom as on the field.

I learned the Royal definition of this "winning education" the first time I talked privately with the brain coach. I had actually been excited about some of my possible courses. Like many my age, the Kennedy administration had given me my first interest in politics.

"I'm thinking about majoring in government and going into politics," I told him, "and I really don't know what to start off with. What is this Government 302L about?" (Advanced government course offered only for freshmen.) "Government 302L . . . let me see." Hewlett turned around and looked in his files. "Not a lot of our boys have taken that course, but it looks like a fine class."

"What's it about?"

"International politics," he said, reading the brief course description that went with it.

"Well. What kind of class is it?" I asked again.

"Most of our boys have seemed to like it. They've done real well. No one has made lower than a C, and if you are going to major in government it fits one of the three electives you're going to have to take."

"No, I mean what do they get into? What do we study?" About this time Hewlett started getting restless and irritated, fidgeting around, and I started getting a little uncomfortable myself.

"Dr. Soukup is a fine professor, and I think you'll like his course," was Hewlett's response as he gave me a restless look that said, "Now let's move on."

But I really wanted to know something about the course, and it was the first time I'd talked to him. So even though I was getting very nervous, I continued.

"Does he have discussion groups or is it all lecture?"

Hewlett was always so controlled, but on this occasion I could see how pissed he was getting. He went over to his files and got out a piece of paper and brought it back and set it in front of me. "Now this is what you'll have to take for government." It was a list of the courses required for a government major.

Obviously, for Hewlett, the only important factor was winning the grades. And he could tell us how to get there— in fact, he always spoke of how well he knew the ins and outs of the university: "Men, I flunked out of this place once before myself, but I got back in a second time to graduate. So I think I know about the obstacles you men will be facing."

An example of this "educational expertise" was his handling of the university faculty. He encouraged their full support by allowing selected "inside" glimpses of Royal's program.

One of those privileged was a Texas professor who has taught at the university for over fifteen years, and the recipient of a couple of teaching awards. At first he gave me permission to use his name, but later he decided against it after talking over with his wife and colleagues the various pressures that might be brought to bear on him despite his having tenure. I'll call him Bill.

"When I arrived at the university I'd never really felt part of anything really American," Bill told me. "And because the university gave me my first real opportunity to be a part, I've always felt both a strong attachment and a deep indebtedness to it. This attachment very much extended to the football team. I saw the football players as student-athletes and representatives of our school. Anyway, since I was a kid I've loved football.

"When I was first invited to sit on the benches and meet the coaches and players, I felt connected to the team. Soon I began attending many of the workouts, and became one of the team's biggest boosters. Darrell would say:

" 'Bill, come on down anytime you want, we're more than happy to have you around.' And every time I went to a workout Darrell or one of the other coaches would make a point to come over for conversation. Combining this with the fact that several of the players were in my classes, I began to have a special interest in the team and I also felt that I was of some personal importance to them. I felt flattered by this connection and the special attention that went with it.

"Yet I still thought of the football players as just other students who happened to play football, and at first when the brain coach would call to check on their class progress, I thought nothing of it. That is, until he called me about a star player [now a star professional player] in one of my classes. He asked me if I was sure about his low grade, if there hadn't been a mistake. I said that I was sure, and then he wanted to know if the player could write another paper, do something to improve his grade. I told him that that depended upon the player himself. I very frequently give my students second chances, and consider this a way of learning. Shortly, this player came to me and asked for a chance to rewrite his paper. I said fine.

"He was a poor student, but wrote a paper much better than anything that he had done before. It was sufficiently well written to change his grade.

"A couple of days later Darrell came up to me and thanked me for the changed grade. I responded by saying, 'Well, Freddy wrote an excellent paper.' Darrell drew back with a shocked look on his face, and after recovering, said:

" 'Oh, yow, Freddy can be quite intelligent when he wants to.'

"Right then I knew I'd been taken—that I had allowed myself to believe that the paper was written by someone who obviously couldn't have written it. I also knew that I would never do it again.

"After this incident I received other calls from the brain coach, such as, 'Bill, are you sure Freddy's grade is a C?' 'Of course I'm sure.' 'Well, Darrell sure is counting on Freddy next fall.'

"I was very angered and made it clear. And soon I received no more calls and no more invitations to team functions.

"I have since found it necessary to completely divorce myself from any connections with the football program at Texas. I have realized that my aim of aiding in the education of students is in direct conflict with the football program's aims of bypassing an education. The football program at Texas has absolutely nothing to do with a university's proper function, and I am saddened by the fact that university professors are among those this program smoothly uses to its own ends."

Generally, however, the football program's rapport with the faculty was efficiently enhanced from many less dangerous angles; for example, Royal's policy of inviting a few members of the faculty to sit on our bench at each home game for what they thought was a behind-the-scenes view.

From the Official Longhorn Program of December 5, 1970, Texas v. Arkansas, there is a description of this behind-the-scenes look:

"Three university faculty members have a ring-side seat for this one, and it's a good bet they'll return to the office or classroom Monday with some 'inside' tales that will stay with them a long, long, time.

"It is all part of the program initiated in 1957, by Coach Darrell Royal, to give university professors a look at what goes on when the Longhorns play a football game.

" 'We started this because we want our faculty to know as much as possible about our program. We are dealing with student-athletes, and we wanted them to be more informed as to what we're doing here,' Royal said.

"Over the years more than 200 UT faculty members have been on the sidelines at home games.

" 'They are invited to everything except the huddle,' jokes Lan Hewlett, UT Athletic Academic Counselor.

" 'The day starts Saturday morning with a tour of our facilities at Gregory Gym. Then we go to the hotel where the team stays and join the squad for the pre-game meal,' Hewlett says.

" 'From there the team and the guests go into the team meeting, where generally a last minute look at a film takes place.

" 'When the lights come back on, if they have any athletic background at all, that's when it gets them . . . they really start to get uptight,' Hewlett says, pointing out, 'Our guests range from the curious to the avid fans.'

"Once at the stadium, Hewlett takes the visiting profs on a tour of the facilities at the stadium while the team warms up. The professors sit on the bench during the game, and accompany the team to the dressing room at half-time and for the brief session immediately following the game.

"Professors have always reacted favorably to the visit. Typical comments include:

" 'It was truly a delightful experience . . . I think it's an excellent program and I hope Coach Royal knows how much we faculty members appreciate the opportunity of seeing Number One first hand.'

" '. . . my appreciation for the opportunity to spend last Saturday with the football team meeting coaches and players and getting to see the football activities from the inside. I was very much impressed and learned a good deal.'

" 'If Coach Royal were interested in it, he could have gone into professional football long ago,' says Hewlett. 'He believes strongly in the student athlete, and he wanted this as a reminder to our faculty and the players that this is done in an academic climate within the structure of the University and its goals.' " [2]

One student-athlete to come out of this academic climate was our freshman coach, Pat Culpepper. Culpepper had been All-American both on the field and scholastically. In fact, Royal had once said that Culpepper was exactly like he'd want a son to be. Fittingly enough Culpepper was the first coach to lecture us on the importance of achieving an education.

His initial speech about education came at the end of our first week. "Men, you are at the university for two reasons—and only two reasons—to play football and to get an education. To do these two things you must sacrifice all else, because that's what it will take. And men, I realize that there will be many temptations to take your minds off these objectives, but to be a winner, you must deny yourself. It is a Spartan existence; but for this Spartan life you will be held in special esteem, the campus will look up to you, and you will be part of the Texas football tradition."

We were special. And I did feel pride in the realization of how tough I'd have to be, that the others couldn't go through what I would. "If Culpepper did it—then I could."

When I first saw Culpepper, I thought that this guy couldn't have been an All-American linebacker. "He's too

---

[2] Official Longhorn Program, Dec. 5, 1970; Texas v. Arkansas.

damn small" (only 185 pounds). And when he started talking to us, he pawed the turf like an embarrassed cub, and without daring to look up, mumbled on, hands in his pockets. In fact, his only audible words came right after regular intervals of turning his head to one side and spitting. I felt uncomfortable at how hard it was for him to talk in front of a group. I knew the feeling. But in five minutes I knew—we all knew—why he was an All-American. The most important ability to have in football is the capacity to psyche yourself, and Culpepper could get it up. I guess he'd only needed a warmup because once he got it turned on, he went. And the faster and louder he talked the more he'd spit.

There were a few times in my four years at Texas that I had the flash that neither I nor my teammates knew what the hell we were doing, what we were really a part of. An occasional event or incident would occur that would jolt me and I would become disoriented and confused. This feeling most frequently occurred when Culpepper went into one of his orations.

"Men, when you're going after somebody, I want you to be a Marine [which he had been] charging Iwo Jima. Attack all out! When you're going downfield you're a kamikaze, and you should have no hesitancy about throwing your body into that enemy [Culpepper would throw his arms forward]. And when we're down here on our goalline on defense, I want you to act like the enemy has you on the edge of a cliff and is trying to shove you off that cliff with his bayonet. [Culpepper spits again and then bends down in an attacking position and points to the imaginary cliff behind him.] Now if somebody was trying to push you off a cliff you'd be scratching and biting and clawing and grabbing all the grass you could find. Now every down that we're on defense and our enemy has the ball, that cliff should be right behind you [spit, spit]."

At these times I seemed to experience a momentary mental paralysis and my mind slowly drifted away from the wildness that was Culpepper when he was psyching us for gridiron warfare. War was his constant metaphor when talking football. And I sensed that at anytime he would lose control and unleash this fervor in scattered shots around him. As he grimaced and nervously moved from one leg to the other, I would think of what older players had told me about his playing days. He reportedly put dents in his closet door from beating it with his forearm, with increasing tempo as game day neared. Supposedly this was to toughen his forearms as well as help him get his psyche up for that week's game. And now, at the slightest excuse, he would use this psyche to give us a personal demonstration on the field.

In fact, the very first day in pads I got a taste of one of these demonstrations. I had just made a tackle and was getting up when Culpepper started coming at me with all that waving of his arms and screaming what he would do. I wasn't used to it yet, and I instinctively reacted just as if a growling dog was running toward me. I got down in a crouch—I couldn't hear anything he was saying. I thought just for a second he was really going to hit me. He didn't stop coming until he was in my face.

"What are you doing? What are you doing! Letting a man smaller than you run over you. When you tackle a man he's got to go backwards. That's the way we play here!"

While he was screaming at me, he kept moving, spitting,

kicking the turf. Yet none of his actions seemed theatrical. He was absolutely sincere.

"Now don't you ever let a man smaller than you run over you again. Get over there and tackle him again."

Culpepper's explosiveness was combined with extreme religiousness which wouldn't let him say anything worse than "dead gum." When he got angry, his eyes seemed to light his dark face a bright red, and I could sense how much effort he was using to get the necessary words out without cursing. Only twice did I ever hear him say "shit," and both times he was flustered to the point of being otherwise unable to speak. And he approached everything the same way. Education was to be attacked just like football. For Culpepper the battle lines had to be clearly drawn as he seemed incapable of tolerating any ambiguity.

When he went into one of his frequent messianic speeches, my immediate response was to half-duck my head. And though all of us would be just quietly standing around him, he never really looked at any of us. It was like he was giving himself a pep talk. But I still attempted to listen, and tried to feel that his ravings were natural, part of what it meant to be really dedicated.

Yet every once in a while I'd notice a guilty grin on some of my teammates' faces, and I'd have trouble keeping from laughing. But these smiling lips were upsetting as they conflicted with my belief in total dedication. So I eliminated this conflict by telling myself that Culpepper was weird, but that his dedication wasn't. Yet I couldn't help wonder how much like him I'd have to be.

Even with my initial doubts about Culpepper I was determined to be completely dedicated to both football and school. If I wasn't on the field or in class, I was studying. And any time I strayed from these duties I felt immediately guilty. In fact, there was only about thirty minutes during the day when I felt free from my discipline. This was the half-hour interval between leaving my last class and going to the field house. This was the most valued time of my freshman year. In this brief thirty minutes I had one place to which I always escaped, one place where I felt completely free but secure. It seems rather ludicrous now, but my best moments as a freshman Longhorn were spent at the same time every day, in the same toilet stall, and on the same john. And I am thoroughly convinced that being able to lock that stall, and then sit and read a magazine in total privacy for thirty minutes each day, enabled me to survive that first year.

My Culpepper-like dedication to disciplined study lasted until the middle of my second semester and then suddenly collapsed. From this point until I graduated I usually concerned myself with finding the shortest routes to the end results. And like most of my teammates, I began going to any lengths to avoid studying. There wasn't a coach standing over me or a Culpepper exhorting me, and my desire to escape another test of my winning character became at times almost frenetic.

So far as we were concerned, our education was just another external measure. And so most of us, including myself, became interested in finding the easy courses rather than the stimulating ones. At times it seemed as if all of us were in the same registration lines as the word quickly got around: "Shaw, take Smith, he gave nothing lower than a B last year." Access to these crib courses was aided by the fact that we had the advantage of registering before the other students, so that our afternoons would be left open for football.

Unfortunately, any number of other means to our ends, including cheating, came to be widely used and pretty much accepted, or at best ignored. For example, as campus celebrities we had access to any number of files (fraternities were especially patronizing to athletes in this way) and we used them. I knew of several teammates just on our freshman team whose work was done largely by girlfriends. Being a football player made this fairly easy to do as there was always a supply of women adulators ready to help. Several of us would be in the same class and a couple of players would get friendly with one of our girl classmates and would manipulate her until all of their class notes came directly from her. Then these players would pass her notes around to the rest of us. Of course, the real prize was to get a girl who would take the risk of letting you have easy access to her answer sheet come exam time. There was one starting star player who as far as I know never wrote one paper or did one homework assignment in his four years —his girlfriend did every single bit of his work.

Of course, a few times in somewhat ironic fashion these practices backfired. In particular, I knew of a reserve half-back who was staying off scholastic probation simply by the good graces of his girlfriend's aid. They had several well-developed cheating systems worked out where she would copy her answers, and they worked these systems in his three most difficult classes. I watched them at work in one, a chemistry class we all had together. Our tests were multiple choice, and in these cases she crossed her legs if the answer was "A," crossed her hands if "B," and put her hand to her face if "C." And they had it worked out how much time she was to take between each answer. It was successful enough that he had a healthy 85 average. But then two days before our chemistry final they had a huge fight and broke up. He didn't have time to find anyone else. He proceeded to make the amazing score of 6, and I'm not sure how he even managed that. He flunked the course and went on scholastic probation, but the next semester he and his girlfriend were back together and so were his grades.

I think many of us came to feel that this assistance was part of our female friends' natural function. It somehow seemed our prerogative, part of the reward we got for our sacrifices. And besides, making the grades and the degree were what counted. In fact, those who were most successful in manipulating their courses and girls into acceptable grades semed proud of it.

Coach Royal, of course, would have said he was against our cheating, but whether he was or not, it was basically not in conflict with his exclusive emphasis on end results.

However, I soon discovered that some end results were much more important than others. It seemed that the minimum end requirements for school often varied according to our football status. The education of those below the third team was much more important to Royal than the education of his starters. Those on the first two teams, and I assure you, not because they weren't cutting classes, didn't seem to need the mental stimulation of running the stands. Because behind the importance of our discipline and regimentation was something much more basic—our football performance itself. Thus, the attendance sheets that we turned in to Hewlett were used very selectively. If a player was doing well in football and there were no problems with his eligibility, he really didn't have to worry about running the stands. But woe to those not doing well on the field, especially during spring drills. If it was spring training, those that ran the stands would, coincidentally enough, usually be the same ones included in special run-off drills during a workout that were to determine a player's real desire to be a Longhorn. Since running the stands had to meet the arbitrary satisfaction of Medina, many of these players had to do it several mornings in a row, which, of course, increased the likelihood of their missing more classes and continuing in the same cycle.

Only once did I ever have to run these stands, at the beginning of spring training my third year. And, coincidentally enough, due to missing almost the entire previous fall, I had started this particular spring training below the third team. My punishment was for missing one class in which I was making an A at the time. Since I had a B average my three previous years of schooling, I don't think Coach Royal was too worried about my grades.

We had had our first spring workout the day before, and when my alarm went off at four-thirty A.M., I had to use every bit of will power my football mind could muster to force my bruised body out of bed. It was still pitch black out and the dorm was noiseless. Going to face my educational discipline, I could see the outline of Texas's Memorial Stadium standing alone in the early morning air. When I walked into the dressing room, Medina was ready to go.

"Son, get your gear on. You have ten minutes." My gear included a twenty-pound-weight vest as well as ankle and wrist weights.

Perhaps strangely, my thoughts were on the coming

afternoon. I was wondering how I would get enough sleep
for our regular spring workout. "I'll cut my fourth-period
class; it doesn't take roll, that'll give me an hour."

"Hurry up son, hurry up, we don't have all morning."
There were a few other disciplinees in the locker room
getting dressed, and this made me feel a little better.

It was a new experience for me to try and psyche myself
this early in the morning, but I knew I had to take it in
stride. If Medina thought he was getting to me, I knew
that I'd have to go that much longer.

Most of the time in workouts I could numb myself,
get my body operating almost automatically, mechanically.
But goddamn, that morning wind blowing in my face while
I ran to the top of that stadium made me very aware of
my legs, my breathing, and the ankle and chest weights
on my body. I was so conscious of running that I almost
couldn't hear Frank yelling, "Put out men . . . put out.
Let's see what you've got," especially when I got to the top
steps of the stadium and could see Austin and its capitol
building in the shadowed distance. Up and down, up and
down. Medina never stopped. When the guy next to me
slipped and fell, he expanded his harangue.

Forty-five long minutes after we had begun, Medina's
exercises began to subside, so I figured we were close to
the end. But about then, my legs started pulling heavy on
my sides, and I knew I was going to have to puke. I just
made it to the top again, where Frank couldn't see me, and
I unloaded. I realized then that there was no way that I
could spend many mornings like this and still make it
through spring training. As I walked back to the dorm
with the sun coming up, I wondered how "Daddy D"
thought this would help me raise my A.

If we did well in both football and education or poorly in both, the reasons would be attributed to the same element of character, discipline (or the lack of it). For example, I've heard Royal, in talking about Culpepper who did well in each, claim that the same character traits were responsible. So in this way our school performance was just another way of measuring a winning character.

Yet ironically, while Royal spoke of the high correlation between "winning" football players and "winning" students, many of his starters were below-average students. Thus, if I was doing well on the field, I would not be considered less a man if I did poorly in the classroom. Yet, if I did well in school and poorly on the field, the judgment would still be made on my field performance. My good grades in this case would be the result of a good mind, but not character. I wouldn't be a winner, just smart. So if I wasn't doing well in football I was in a situation where I couldn't win. By screwing up in school, my negative value would go even further down; but it would not really go up much if I did well. So my only reason to make the grades would be to keep from being a bigger shit than I already was.

Thus, as long as we were doing well in football, we were considered to have some character and value, no matter what else we did. And for these valuable players, "the brain coach has one objective: To keep the Texas athlete in school." [3] For them, Hewlett's tutoring program was used to the full. And often these tutors (usually graduate students being paid by the athletic department) did more than make suggestions. In fact, the teacher with some jurisdiction over these tutors (now a professor in the Texas English

---

[3] *Darrell Royal Talks Football*, p. 196.

department) finally had to blow the whistle when it became flagrantly obvious how far their aid really extended. It included such help as the actual writing of term papers. And if these valuable players were still having grade problems, they were encouraged to stretch their education out. For them there was nothing magical about graduating in four years. Indeed, nearly every starter on Texas's 1963 National Champions did not.

But when our football performances slipped, so did academic aid. For example, a borderline player could expect practically no help from Hewlett. Wayne Suttle fell into this category. "Hewlett never gave me any help at all, absolutely no advice or consultation. I'd ask him about a course and he'd say, 'Take anything you want.' Shit, he was a farce."

But the guys in real hot water were those who were not doing well on the field and also had poor grades. Here there were further subtle gradations in Hewlett's help and response. In this case, Hewlett seemed more insistent that these players stay on a course having them graduate in four years. Not that he would intentionally flunk the guys, just that he would discourage the taking of a couple of grade-point courses, and would give lectures on the sins of taking the easy way out. "If you give in that easily, how do you ever expect to make the team?"

I remember in particular one big jovial teammate who played my position, guard. He was from a small Texas town with one country school, and he was having trouble with his grades. In fact, he was on scholastic probation. But worse yet, despite fanatical effort, he just wasn't panning out on the football field. After seeing Hewlett about his second spring registration, he came into my room somewhat angry and upset, but more puzzled than anything else. "Shaw, look at the shit Hewlett has me taking, goddamn economics. Man, look at this book." He stuck out his newly bought economics book. At that time economics had a high percentage of flunks. "He told me to sign up for all this or I was going to get behind. He wouldn't let me take that P.E. course Helms was taking, said it wouldn't help me."

This guy was in trouble scholastically, and yet here he was signed up for five tough courses, a full load. This was with spring training coming and five or six weeks where none of us would be able to give even meager attention to our studies. I knew right then that he was going to flunk out. Yet I didn't feel particularly bad about it. That was just the way things were. In fact, by my second year it was a joke among some of us that everyone should go to Hewlett, he'd show you the quickest, most efficient way to flunk out.

Usually whenever I found out that one of my teammates was having scholastic problems, especially if he was a lineman and any good, I'd secretly be glad. I'd wonder when he'd be gone, and I even remember figuring out on paper who my competition would be the next year and what their chances were of making it scholastically. I remember how elated I was my third year (sophomore athleticwise) when I found out a guy I was battling for second team had left school because of bad grades. To me it was just another way of mowing down competition.

And indeed, it seemed that my teammates were always disappearing. There were forty-four of us signed to a full scholarship the year I came to Texas. By my fourth year there were only eleven of us left. There was great pride in being one of the survivors, even if the casualties were due to scholastic difficulties. We felt there was something lacking in those who left. When anyone quit, the rest of us would count up the number that had departed and how many that left in our class. These revised stats were a source of nervous enthusiasm and conversation for days.

Of course, none of us remaining dared mention our own doubts and personal thoughts about leaving. Underneath I always felt some vague fear, especially when someone left who I didn't expect to go. It was a fear that was ever present, but that I tried to keep forced into the background. It almost seemed like some infectious disease from which I had to guard against constantly. And it was most important to give myself the proper mental medicine, especially when I was down, or else I would fall casualty to the worst thing that one could be, a quitter.

But by my second year I wanted to try and fit a few things other than football into our academic climate. I was becoming aware and interested in some of the Texas campus's myriad activities. It was the year of the Johnson-Goldwater election, and the Young Democrats were involved with Johnson. I decided I wanted to join, but I quickly discovered that there was no way that I could actively participate. Spring training was starting so I couldn't work for them during the afternoons because of our workouts. Nor could I attend their evening meetings because we had to watch films at night.

Yet the little contact I had with these students exposed me to stimulation that was basically alien and unavailable in my Moore-Hill world. They would talk about some movie festival at the campus union, or a well-known lecturer speaking on Wednesday evening, or a discussion group they were in Tuesday night, and for the first time I was becoming aware that all this was part of what I, as a football player, was missing. Coach Royal had always bragged about the fact that his football players' grade-point average was higher than the grade-point average of the student body as a whole; yet I began to wonder just how much more than making the grade was involved in an education.

But getting out of my tight enclosure was even physically difficult. During our first two years we couldn't live outside the athletic dorm, and we could move out after that only with Coach Royal's personal permission. He wanted us to all live together. He felt that there were too many temptations if we were separated and left to other influences. So my only recourse was to try and find some mental activity where I was. My desire was to relate in some way not structured by the fact that I was a football player, but most of my teammates were totally anti-intellectual, and not necessarily because of lack of brains. Part of the mold of being the sort of guy that's tough enough to be a winner meant that there were only certain things that we could talk about. These were generally sports, but not how they affected us; sex, but not how we felt; and stories about one another, but never very revealing. Any effort I made to be something outside of this structure was met with avoidance and nervousness. To talk about politics, religion, or anything of substance had nothing to do with what it meant to be a man, so why get into it?

Though sexual exploits were often a favorite dorm topic, they were never discussed in a way that gave any indication of real feeling for the girl involved. For example, one of my teammates got very explicit pictures and letters from his girlfriend regularly. These were sensational bits of evidence that he was scoring in a dramatic fashion, and he showed us these badges proudly. Almost immediately after a letter arrived, about ten of us would be crowded into his room. Like kids with candy, we fought over the pages as we discussed his "ultimate touchdown." For most of us, our discussions of our feelings never got past the point of scoring.

And for me, pursuing any knowledge out of its own intrinsic delight was quickly removed from my experience. True, to some degree, this probably happened to most other non-football students. But the relative degree of this intense preoccupation with making it, the grades, to the exclusion of all else seemed significantly greater with us jocks. Even the brighter players who were very sensitive to the stereotyped mode of "dumb jock" couldn't seem to escape this driving motivation. The way they fought the stereotyped football mold was to make better grades than the rest of us. And I gradually came to get my psyche up for studying the same way I got it up for workouts. When studying late for a test, comments such as "It's fourth quarter, I've got to suck it up," were common to all of us.

I was in a mental straitjacket and didn't know how to get out. I would sporadically try to get into other activities or read a few books on my own, but this always made me feel as if I was running from my contests. Besides, to pursue something out of positive genuine interest was scary; I was leaving my familiar framework. Outside of this framework there were no coach's guidelines and no support. And like a babe I would crawl back for cover. Our coaches would tell us about the necessity for self-discipline, but what they really meant was obedience. Real self-discipline requires independence and self-reliance and the capacity to choose as well as pursue individual aims.

Yet having coaches almost completely run our lives

wasn't the tension-free existence you might expect it to be. With this discipline went constant pressure as they also determined how we were to measure up and if we had. And in this way my teammates on the whole were the most docile people I've ever known. Most had seemed to accept the fact that coaches and other authorities were to make all their decisions. The only way to avoid the heaviest part of this pressure was to be making it in football, and in my initial spring training, I wasn't.

In the first two weeks of these spring drills my whole world semed to disintegrate. I started off running second team, but slipped to fourth. Not only was I not a star, the coaches didn't even call me by name. Then midway through the spring I was hurt (blood-clotting in my arm) and missed all the remaining workouts. Within days after my injury I seemed to lose all my drive. I began wanting to be as unobtrusive and unnoticed as possible. Since we had football meetings practically every evening during spring training (the injured still had to go to workouts and films), I had gotten three or four weks behind in school. To catch up I was really going to have to hump it. But even after spring training ended I couldn't seem to turn it on, and I started finding it difficult to even get up and attend class.

About a month before the semester was over I started think I must be sick because I had no energy and I couldn't make myself study. I knew that if I didn't start quickly there was no way that I could make it. But five days before finals were to start, I still hadn't begun studying, and I checked into the student health center.

I was in three days when I called my parents and told them I was dropping out on account of illness. They were very upset and told me, "Gary, if you quit now, you'll always be a quitter."

I left the hospital and studied day and night. With plenty of luck, I struggled through with a D in French and a C average. Afterward, I felt that I'd been saved, just as in the eighth grade, and that I still had a chance to prove myself a winner.

Suttle

When a player left the team, he usually quit school too. When Wayne Suttle left no one saw him leave, and like the others that followed, I never heard his name or departure mentioned by the coaching staff.

"Nobody ever said a word to me except Hewlett," Wayne told me. "He called and told me to be sure and turn in my student ID card."

Wayne Suttle came from a large city right in the heart of Texas. Although Waco has a hundred thousand people you'd swear you were in a small, one Dairy Queen town. Waco High is one of the oldest high schools in Texas and has been long known for its football, with glory days dating back to national and state championships in the twenties.

In Wayne's senior year, Waco High was reputed to have some of the finest talent in the state. Wayne wasn't the biggest star on his team nor was he considered a Blue Chipper, but he was considered a good enough prospect to be widely recruited. He was six foot three and lanky, looking a little as if someone had decided to assemble the perfect football package but hadn't gotten around to adding that beefy quality that identifies you as "football player." Coach Royal always liked to recruit this kind of player, lean and hungry, and I think he must get pleasure in participating in the final construction, adding that "longhorn" meat and muscle. The last and winning touches.

Wayne told me that the first thing Royal even said to him—as to most of us—was something about his body. "He came up to me at a track meet in my senior year in high school and said, 'Hi, Wayne, how much do you weigh now?'

I'd only seen pictures of him and I didn't even know who he was."

Wayne was strikingly good-looking with dark hair, brown eyes, and an All-American smile. Although he looked like the sophisticated New York playboy, his mellow country twang and unassuming ways quickly laid that image to rest. This country ease included a kind of innocent schoolboy humor that loved to talk about "farts and fuckin'."

Wayne seemed less driven than the rest of us. He never seemed to be able to put his own importance and that of "making it" at the very apex of the universe. As a result he was well-liked by all, but too easygoing to be associated with by most of us more hard-driven ones. We couldn't afford to be around someone like Wayne who was not in the Texas mold. But even with his relative easiness, Wayne at the same time conveyed a seriousness that was very rare in our "tough" world. His eyes betrayed him and gave away a different and alien kind of feeling, a mellowness and softness that would sneak through even when he was attempting to speak roughly. In most of our eyes if any gaze came through other than one that befits a football player, always moving, aggressive, on the make, it was a glimmer of being lost and bewildered; but one had to look hard for this, and it was fleeting. Solid gazes were not to be found except an occasional hard, determined one that showed courage and perseverance. Whatever the reason, Wayne's brown eyes lacked this defensiveness.

Instinctively, I knew there was something different about him, though his actions and roughhouse ways were generally no different from the typical jock's. He made bad grades, got drunk a lot, and talked mostly about screwing girls. In fact, Wayne looked most natural sitting down and drinking a cold Coors and telling dirty jokes.

Wayne, though affable, was pretty much a loner. He'd say and do what he wanted and, though not a leader, was definitely not a follower. His main circle of friends was limited to three or four other average players.

What happened to Wayne at Texas and his relationship or nonrelationship with Royal was typical. Wayne seemed an average player who tried pretty hard, though not in the killer "rah-rah" style. They played him at tackle where he was second and third team on the freshman squad and ran fourth team his first spring on the varsity. The next fall he was red-shirted but by December he was gone.

What went on during that time? How often did he see Royal? What did he think of him?

Fact number one is that Wayne had only two conversations with Royal in his entire association, only one of which Royal initiated. The first was the one mentioned, when Wayne was a senior in high school and Royal asked him about his weight. This was the singular instance in Wayne's memory that Royal ever approached him. The second instance occurred the day before Wayne left school. In between he never shared another word with "Daddy D."

Wayne was for the most part one of many borderline players. It seemed as though he could just as easily make it as not. The first spring he was running as high as most of us first-year men, until the last week. Then came the turning point that Wayne remembers well.

"It was the spring game and I heard Coach Coffee [one of the line coaches] yelling, 'Suttle! Suttle! Goddamnit, where's Suttle?' I had been feeling ill all day and had not expected to play. Upon hearing my name I simply looked up and waited for my orders. When I didn't jump up, Coach Coffee went into a rage. He screamed 'To hell with Suttle, he doesn't want to play football.' From that point on it was never the same."

The coaches expected a player to be ever ready. At the sound of your name you were to be leaping to the side of the beckoning coach. We had to be always properly enthusiastic because they had a large supply of others ever "ready and willing."

Suttle's position quickly deteriorated. When he came back for two-a-days in the fall he was on one of the lower teams, and the coaches started riding him. During the season he found himself occasionally running the stands at five in the morning and otherwise being totally ignored except for occasional verbal cuts. They don't have "shit drills" during the season, but he would have been one of the participants had he lasted until spring. However, his tolerance for shit was less than most of us, and an incident in December of 1964 caused his early departure.

We were 9-1 that year and had accepted an invitation to the Orange Bowl to play Joe Namath and Alabama. As a redshirt Suttle had been working out all year on the scout team and naturally expected to go to Miami with the rest of the squad. The coaches posted a list of who could go and who couldn't. Wayne was not allowed to go, while included on the list of who could go were several players who had been injured and hadn't even worked out. And the final kicker was that even though Wayne wasn't getting to go to Miami, he was to work out with the team all through the Christmas holidays. No reasons or explanations were given, but it was clear they wanted his scholarship.

This was one of the many tools at Royal's disposal to humiliate and convince someone that it wasn't worth it. "I was so embarrassed to be singled out like that. I knew everyone else had seen the list," Wayne told me.

It was clear to the rest of us that Suttle was a marked man. Most of us would have been angered at this pointed embarrassment, but would have been too afraid to do anything about it. But Wayne was stronger and more independent than the great majority of us, so he and three others left off the Miami list went to see Coach Royal. Wayne did the talking for the players, what little of it there was. If there is one thing Coach Royal doesn't like, it's a player giving the slightest hint of questioning his authority.

"I was nervous, but I said, 'Coach, I think we're kinda getting screwed around by not getting to go to Miami.' Boy, that pissed Royal off. Immediately he got all red in the face and he leaned over his desk and said, 'Suttle, nobody is screwing you around—period.' I felt like the breath had been sucked out of me. I just kinda froze. I don't even remember anything about the rest of the conversation. None of the other guys said anything."

Wayne had played the strong-man part through all this and tried to act unaffected. "Fuck 'em. They're not going to screw me over like this," were his typical responses. Even before things had started getting progressively worse for him, he had given the impression that he would stand up and not be jacked around. And the month before going to see Royal, he had become increasingly adamant in his toughness, at least in front of us. However, toward the end I could see him approaching his "high noon," without a six-shooter. The next day after his second and final "conversation" with Royal, he left Texas for good.

In some ways, the rest of us admired Wayne for seeming to stand up for his rights. The general feeling was that "Suttle wouldn't take all that shit." But at the same time there was the unexpressed but more strongly felt thought that he just couldn't take it, he was one of "those people" who were quitters. Because stand up or not, "a quitter was a quitter."

The first thing Wayne did after leaving Texas was to get

in contact with some other schools about playing football. He got several offers, and his old high school coach encouraged him to take another four-year scholarship. "I'd never quit anything before and this seemed the only way to redeem myself." He thought about it for a month, and then realized that he really didn't want to play.

"All I'd ever been was a football player, and I didn't know what else to do. Then came the low point of my life. My high school coach was constantly bugging me and everyone kept asking me what happened at Texas."

Wayne worked in factories and other low-paying jobs for two years in Waco. At the end of the first year he told his high school coach, "I never want you to mention football to me again, so quit bugging me." At that point he decided "never to tell anyone again that I'd played football at Texas." Wayne told me that most of the people who know him now would be shocked to find out that he'd once played college football. "Now I hardly ever even watch a football game on TV."

What does he remember about Texas? I asked him if he felt he had learned anything from the coaches or remembered anything they'd told him. "The only thing I remember," he said, "is a talk Royal gave us:"

" 'Men, this is a football field. [Royal draws a rectangle on the board.] We don't care what happens between the two twenty-yard lines. But everything inside the twenties is ours. The rest doesn't matter.'

"That's all I remember that any of the coaches said to us, and I don't know why I remember that.

"Quitting was the hardest thing I ever did. I wondered what everyone thought of me. I didn't want to see them again. No way I could stay around with them knowing that I'd quit. I just couldn't have eaten at the dorm."

"Why didn't you just quit and still keep your scholarship?"
I asked him.

"I really didn't know I could keep my scholarship. I
really didn't think about that shit until afterwards. But I
wasn't about to stay around Moore-Hill and have others
see me, or go into that dining room again."

"What are your feelings about Royal?"

"Not much one way or the other. I doubt that Royal would
remember my name. I don't think I was any more to him
than a wooden peg."

"Did you like any of the coaches?"

"Yeah, Coach Shira." (Defensive line coach now at
Mississippi State.)

"What about him did you like?"

"He didn't yell, and always called me by my first name.
I always tried to put out extra for him."

"Do you think that you got anything out of football?"

A shrug of the shoulders and no response.

"Did you in any way like playing college football?"

"Shit no."

"Why did you play as long as you did then?"

"I don't know why I did it—I don't know what kept me
going."

Wayne just finished getting his degree at North Texas
State in Denton and is finally working on a job he likes. It
took him several years, but he said he thought he'd now dis-
associated himself from the idea of being a football player.
"Only in the last year did I stop feeling that I *had* to go to
the very top in my business."

This statement comes from one of the least driven members of the team. Wayne was in no way as caught up in
proving himself a winner as the great majority of us. Yet it
has taken him nearly eight years to feel really free from the

"winning is all" football mentality experienced at Texas.

Out of the forty-four who went to Texas in the fall of 1963, over three-fourths of us left before that fourth year. While most of those departing went through at least what Wayne did, not many had his independence and strength. I wonder how many of them have managed to separate themselves from these experiences.

Finally, I asked Wayne what he hated most about his football experiences at Texas. "Those damn Medina sessions! Those have been the hardest things for me to push out of my mind."

Medina Sessions

If I were required to indicate today that element of American life which is most characteristic of our nationality, my finger would unerringly point to our athletic escutcheon.

—General Douglas MacArthur

When we don't use our ability to the fullest, we're not only cheating ourselves and the Green Bay Packers, we're cheating the Lord. He gave us our ability to use to the fullest.

—Vince Lombardi

Pride is a sense of worth derived from something that is not organically part of us, while self-esteem derives from the potentialities and achievements of the self. We are proud when we identify ourselves with an imaginary self, a leader, a holy cause, a collective body or possessions. There is fear and intolerance in pride; it is sensitive and uncompromising. The less promise and potency in the self, the more imperative is the need for pride. The core of pride is self-rejection.

—Eric Hoffer

"Some of you men will make it and some of you won't. We are here to separate the men from the boys." Frank Medina always walked back and forth. Each rigid step a separate existence. A white towel was carefully drawn around his neck. He was a caricature of seriousness. I never remember him smiling during one of his training sessions. Though Medina gave us basically the same speech at each of his sessions, he always spoke with dramatic intensity as if we were hearing it for the first time.

Medina was a squatty, bowlegged, five-foot-tall Cherokee Indian. He was considered one of the best trainers in the country, and had been a United States Olympic trainer; justifiably so since he was good at the specific duties connected with being a trainer. He could tape ankles, aid in rehabilitation from football injuries, and he knew a lot about physical conditioning. But like most of Royal's helpers, his duties didn't stop with job specifics. His most important contribution was aiding in the developing of our football mentality.

For this last duty he was delegated substantial power. He supervised the running of the stands at five in the morning, he made decisions about the seriousness of injuries, including giving permission to see a doctor, and he conducted "Medina sessions." This was the name we players gave the pre- and post-spring training exercises he supervised. These were for all freshmen and second- and third-year men Royal was interested in running off. The drills themselves lasted only an hour to an hour and a half, but we had good reason for sometimes calling them "torture drills." They started at the beginning of the second semester and stopped when spring training began six weeks later.

78

Supposedly these Medina sessions tested our worth. And ideally for Medina and the coaches, being a man and thus worthwhile only involved the personal qualities for becoming a good football player. This kind of identity included a few specific characteristics and excluded all else. One, we were to be completely dedicated to our tasks, with of course, unquestioned physical courage. More importantly, we were to convince Medina and the coaches that we could take punishment and deny ourselves for a future goal. Most importantly, we had to eliminate any doubts in their minds that we might ever give up something we had begun; that we would ever quit. When we tried to prove this worth in Medina sessions with Medina screaming in our ears, most of us did what Wayne Suttle did. "I just tried not to think of anything. I just got it in my head that as long as that son-of-a-bitch yelled, I wasn't going to quit. I just blocked everything out. I knew if I let them get to me then they'd try to break me by having me running those goddamned stands."

This threat of punishment reinforced our total dedication and tacitly demanded that we should never question our coaches' authority. Like good soldiers, our job was to follow orders, not think about them. And if we ever did question these values, we were putting ourselves in the arrogant position of thinking we might know more about ourselves than they. Yet, if the coaches or Medina ever questioned our performance, they were questioning our manhood.

No wonder so many football players compare the game of football to the game of life. Football, by its own definition, is a test that separates men from boys. In fact, for many players it is a misnomer to say football is like life—it is life. But if you are a coach who is only interested in winning football games, you want to minimize any feelings, desires, or interests that might interfere or supersede these few qualities. And the more Coach Royal could maximize the importance of these few characteristics and connect them to being a football player, the more likely he was to win.

I'm not suggesting that Royal went through this thinking process when trying to make us better football players. But he knew that the more we measured ourselves on these terms, the more important football would become. And any way that he could control our environment by making us think of ourselves as football players first and foremost, the more successful he would be. Supporting this control was the fact that all the coaches, trainers, most older players, and the brain coach believed in and accepted this world as the one defining one. They had measured themselves that way, and believed in measuring us the same way.

Thus, for all of us at seventeen and eighteen, our complete world was evaluating us only on these terms. And in the process, these few terms got whittled down even further; we made it as a football player or we didn't, we won or we lost. There wasn't a second place. And actually every one of us lost because even to make it left our being shriveled and completely subject to their external control. So if football made men out of us, as Daddy D claimed, it was mechanical men with a single opening for feelings. And as tough, dedicated robots that wouldn't quit, we had to force all our humanity out of this one narrow hole, if it was to come out at all.

Clearly Royal could not be the coolly detached final overseer and judge of our success, while at the same time be fervently and daily imbibing these values. Thus, many people and much time were needed to supply our tightly controlled environment. Beneath Royal, and more dedicated to systematically convincing us of this identity and way of life, were his helpers, like Culpepper, Hewlett, and Frank Medina.

We reported to Medina the first week in January. We had heard endless discussion about Medina sessions from second- and third-year men, but most of us passed these off as exaggerated. These drills took place in two locker rooms that were closed off from where we dressed. Our attire for these affairs was one or two sweat suits, wrist weights, ankle weights, a twenty- to thirty-pound vest, and in each hand we were to carry a thirty-pound dumbbell.

After dressing the first day, Medina called us through the closed doors. The steam heaters in these two rooms pushed the temperature to 120 degrees.

"Sit down, men, and I call you men . . . because you are men." This was the same sentence, word for word, that he started every one of his speeches with. We soon found out that all these sessions included a thirty- to forty-minute oratory prior to the workout.

"Men, why do you think Texas is a champion? . . . A winner? . . . [full fifteen-second pause] . . . I'll tell you why, men . . . [another pause] because we only have winners . . . [five second pause] and champions play for the University of Texas. Your coach . . . [long pause] . . . Coach Royal . . . is a champion . . . and . . . and you must be a champion to play for him Some of you men will make it . . . [full ten-second pause] . . . and some of you will not . . . [longest pause] . . . because you do not have the character, you do not have what it takes. Now men, I'm going to work you and work you . . . because I want to see you become men . . . [long pause] . . . But some of you sitting here will quit . . . [ten second pause] . . . and never make it."

During these excruciatingly long pauses he would be walking in a staccato step. When he spoke it was rapid, until he reached another pause. Every so often his pauses would fall into a regular beat, and I could drift with the "music." But generally his speech was so irregular and harsh, with the pauses so totally unpredictable, that my whole mind stutterred in futile attempts to escape. The beat jabbed . . . jabbed . . . and poked me until I usually felt punchy when the workout finally commenced.

On one hand, we saw Medina as comically pathetic. We frequently made fun of him among ourselves and often daydreamed when he began his oratory. But on the other hand, while we made fun of Frank and his style, we believed nearly all of what he said. And he just kept pounding it in, while we sat there each day listening to it over and over. I wondered sometimes if the steam and heat were to help press his words more indelibly into our naïve minds.

Though not reachable, Frank was at least in some ways tangible. And occasionally a glimmer of affection hurried to my consciousness from quick glances at his dark crusading face. It was always marooned by the pure white of his ever-present towel, and this combination gave him the look of an errant, stubby Don Quixote. We were to be his army of men. Spartan champions that rode off into the night to beat off indolence, softness, indecisiveness and pleasure. Sadly, however, this innocent appeal disappeared with the realization that Medina was a middle-aged man with tremendous power and authority over our lives.

Yet certainly much more than just Frank was in that room, and our eighteen-year-old posteriors were kept to our chairs by more than the weights on our bodies. Could it be that some diluted "American male dream" was fighting strangulation, gasping for air and ventilation in these steam rooms? I could almost imagine our grandfathers' and their grandfathers' images silhouetted against the lockers. These imaginary figures were making sad, painful attempts to tame the wilderness and conquer the West, gallantly riding broken-down ponies. And I could even more easily imagine many of our fathers winning bread for their families and fighting "to free the world for democracy," but now these American he-men and their enemies were fading into the stadium shadows.

This fading past brought tremendous pressure on us. Our confused role was somehow to keep this way of life and its masculine phantasy from dying. The forebears of this tradition had built million-dollar stadiums so that their offspring could play football. Maybe in this way they thought that their heritage would not be forgotten, and they would still know who they were. The support of this male myth had been left to our virile bodies, and betrayal would not be taken lightly.

And to those like Medina, football had obviously become a symbol of the righteous real men of the world. He often talked of the intricate connection between being a good Christian and good football player. He claimed it was impossible to be a good football player without being a good Christian. He was sure of the connection although he never made an effort to explain it. At the most bizarre moments he would speak about being a good Christian man, a champion. In fact, right in the middle of a particularly grueling exercise session, suddenly, without any warning, he asked us if we had attended church the past Sunday. It was an especially disjointing moment for me, as for some reason I had been really aware of my body, its breathing and sweating. It was one of the few times even associated with football that I remember feeling my body as part of me. I had felt as though the water and vapor from my pores were producing a heavy, hard mist that was clearly distinct from the natural steam surrounding me. So when, with no warning, Medina said, "How many of you went to church Sunday?", I was suddenly suspended and separated from any reality. It was so unexpected that I didn't have the mind set even to understand the question, although I did manage an incredulous gasp. Strangely, unless from shock, no one else flinched, smiled, or said a word. Medina then lined us up in a circle, slowly asking again: "Did you go to church Sunday? If you did, raise your hands." Most hands went up but about ten didn't. One of those who didn't raise a hand was Chachie Owens, who had the misfortune to be standing closest to Medina.

"You heathen, come here!" (He really said heathen!) Medina pulled Chachie out of the line. "How do you ever expect to be a champion? To be a football player for the University of Texas? I want you in church Sunday. Do you hear me?"

"Yes, sir."

He then told us that he would ask the same question the following Monday and if we didn't go to church the coming Sunday, there would be disciplinary action taken. Throughout, none of our faces ever changed expression. When he had finished we stood without moving and waited for further orders. The perspiration of my body had dissipated into someone else's moisture, and for a brief moment I thought we must all be crazy. The next Monday he lined us up in another circle and asked again—this time individually. At each stop, we heard, "Yes, sir." Most of us lied.

Medina sessions started off with several minutes of regular calisthenics. Then we began exercises with the dumbbells, first by running with our knees high and the dumb-bells above our heads. We ran in circles, crowded into one room, with the dumbbells moving in an up-down motion. As soon as we stopped running, we were to stand perfectly straight with the barbells held at arms' length from our chest.

"All right, men, today we are going to find out something. Now get those weights out there as far as you can . . . and hold them." This was constant from Frank and three of his student assistants. He conducted these workouts from the top of a bench, which he stalked back and forth, stopping his shouting only for his pauses. His usual policy was to pick out two or three and ride them through the complete work-out.

"All right, Shaw, today I'm going to see what you've got."

Next came jumping jacks, jumping into the air as high as possible, armlifts, situps, and four or five others. Each exercise would continue until someone faltered; for example, couldn't hold the weights up any more. Whoever faltered was made the center of a big production.

"All right, men, it looks like Shaw can't take it today. We're going to have to do these all over again just for him." So everyone would have to go through the whole exercise again, then usually again, sometimes five or six times. Generally, several of us would falter at once, but Medina would pick out one or two and announce that they were responsible for our doing it all over again. I would become enraged at anyone whose name was called, and was always determined that we wouldn't have a repetition because of me. After we had gone long enough, the rest of us would start grumbling and bitching at whoever was "responsible."

"Goddamn, Bledsoe, get off your ass," would come in a

broken unison. And occasionally Frank would pick the same guy out three or four times in a row until some of us were threatening him physically.

After these exercises our sweats would be soaked. Then we went outside the locker rooms to an area under the stadium. Here we had jump-rope races. We lined up in two lines with trainers at each end. Of course, we still had on our weighted vest, wrist and ankle weights. While we were running and jumping, Frank would sometimes run along beside us cramming "commitment" into our ears. "Put out Shaw, put out, hurt yourself, you can run faster than that." Never stopping——I really never understood how all that noise could come from one mouth.

After the jump-rope races, back into the sweat room for more. Again, there was the same series of repetitions with the barbells. One day I especially remember, and it serves as an example. Our last exercise using the dumbbells was situps. Usually we did a hundred at this point (anyone screwed up, we started over). But this day Medina didn't stop at a hundred . . . or two hundred . . . or three hundred . . . nor four hundred . . . five hundred situps with barbells! If five hundred situps doesn't sound like much, try just fifty for yourself without weights, barbells, or forty-five minutes' previous workout in a sweat room. It was close to spring training and we were all in top physical shape. Yet two or three threw up on the concrete and most of us were crying and moaning—the whole time Medina in a separate world atop his bench:

"Men, push yourselves, now's the time to find out . . . (pause) what you've got inside."

The concrete floor had rubbed us raw and most of our butts were bleeding. I was cut enough that I had trouble sitting for two weeks. His three assistant trainers, none of whom weighed over 140 pounds, were parading through the room screaming at us individually.

"Helms, I thought you were tough. Shaw, can't you take it? What's wrong with you guys, how do you ever expect to play for the University of Texas?"

These assistants tried to imitate Frank. He would tell them that "they had to push these men," which is the only excuse they needed for their own personal power trips. These guys were our own age and half our size, yet were towering over us in gleeful domination. But they were protected and they knew it. If we touched them, we would be marked as troublemakers who couldn't take it. The official term was "unable to get with the program."

Next came the punching-bag exercise. This drill, more than any other, epitomized the complete giving of yourself to authority and its instruction. We wore gloves, like those used in golf, and were to box, attacking a big heavy bag that hung from the ceiling. Medina conducted this exercise in a half crouch, perhaps to keep his excitement in the room. It was his favorite drill, and he looked half-maniacal. His hysterical machismo seemed to carry him away from any frustrations into some private world. During these twenty minutes his eyes had enough intensity to carry us with him, not knowing where we were going, but not about to ask.

Each of us did this feat individually and in front of the others.

"Hit it, hit it, I want to hear leather—hit it—let's see your stuff—hit it," as Medina inhaled all air and life surrounding that padded punching bag. We were his; but seemingly insatiable, he grew louder . . . and louder . . . calling for more, more, more. . . . We hit the bag into a shrinking world until it seemed our one friend, and finally we leaned on its broad shoulders and gave only love pats.

"Hit it, you couldn't break an egg. I want to *see* something." And at times someone would fall to the floor from exhaustion.

In this drill Medina's favorite guinea pig was an end named Jim Moses. Moses was the son of a wealthy Houstonite and the younger brother of a former Texas All-American. Jim had relatively little physical ability and the least stamina of anyone on the team. He had no business being on the same field with most of us, but his brother's picture hung on the training-room wall, and he was trying to make it somehow. I could feel the pressure in his body just walking by him. Medina invariably depleted Jim, and he would fall against that bag, a rubbery body loosely wrapping its arms around solace.

"Frank, I can't," and Medina's response was to increase the tempo, as if given his rawest, unformed chance to make a man.

"Hit, Moses, I want something from you, Moses, let's *see* something."

The first week of these drills I thought that other people wouldn't believe me if I simply told them about Medina sessions. They would have to see to believe. I had fantasies of hooking up a hidden camera and recorder. I thought perhaps it could be used for posterity. In the year 2200 they would have a film of American adolescence in the twentieth century: "Yes, this was apparently very typical then. Here we have forty-five boys agreeing to indulge in mutual self-torture and madness for the profit and entertainment of their elders."

However, after a very short time, these Medina episodes didn't seem that strange or unusual. There was much pain; yet somehow these sessions came to have a surreal quality about them. I would feel somewhat detached, dissociated.

At times I even felt like an observer who was slightly amazed at how much my own body could take. And when I saw someone like Moses go through what he did, I usually felt nothing, I just seemed to block it out.

However, there were certain moments of fear, anger, or extreme exhaustion when my cool detachment collapsed. For example, when it was my turn for the punching bag, adrenalin would streak through my body. All those eyes were watching my "maleness" attack that bag. Frank would be circling and screaming, with me between him and the bag. The student trainers were Frank's immediate background and echoed him. Weighing on this were teammates who would yell aborted encouragement in some half-believed attempt at male community. In this drill the rest would urge on whoever was attacking the bag, supposedly encouraging more frantic effort. But perhaps it was really an attempt to add some kind of harmony and consistency to our own actions. During these moments I'd feel half-crazed. All our personalities seemed to immerse in Frank's until the room was speaking with a voice that was neither his nor ours.

After the punching bag we put on the gloves for three rounds of shadow-boxing. In this we worked in pairs. One would hold his gloves apart, the other would pound them. Then we would alternate. The whole time we were to keep moving in boxing style. By this time we were so exhausted that we would often miss, hitting one another in the face.

It was during this shadow-boxing that I broke for the first time. I was having trouble standing, but was still swinging. Frank had been riding me all during the session and was on top of the bench drilling my ears.

"What's wrong, Shaw, what's wrong with you?"

Suddenly, in one smooth, full frenzy I wheeled, lunged, and swung for him. He had just turned his back and was walking the other way as my glove and scholarship whisked by the back of his head—barely missing. I was raising my other to follow the first when my boxing partner grabbed me. Immediately I snapped back—I realized what I had done. I was trembling, and all I could think of was how close I'd come to blowing it. Frank and most of the others hadn't seen me swing, but it scared me enough that I didn't come close to snapping again for two years. I often thought of this instance, and it helped me keep a vigil on myself.

While Medina was a man-eating tiger in our drills, he was a young schoolboy with the coaches. As much as he growled for us, he smiled for them, and he put in a lot of yes sirs and no sirs. With Royal his brown eyes were gracious and polite, and he acted the loyal servant. Royal probably liked Medina's gung-ho efficiency, but he gave the impression that his regard for Medina stopped there.

Like Culpepper, Medina struck me as a fanatic and I made fun of his actions, while thinking that they had no effect on me. Yet at the same time, I believed what he basically espoused. This inconsistency led to my gradually seeing his actions not as so fanatical or abnormal. This was my way of dealing with the inconsistency. I couldn't see that the whole program's total emphasis on a few values was inseparable from some form of fanaticism. Most others, I think, went through a similar resolution. And once we started accepting these actions as normal, we were moving toward the perfect football mentality. That is, the football fanatic whose total existence and worth is dependent on his football performance. Also, I felt that whatever these people said and did must have a good reason, must be right; how could so many be wrong? Who was I to question Darrell Royal and his staff? Maybe I just couldn't take it and was looking for an excuse to quit, was one of "those." This kind of thinking helped me become even more accustomed to discounting my immediate responses.

Medina sessions served as our initiation rite, our first real taste of what was expected. Most second-year men and above didn't go through Medinas. They were either gone or they had acclimated themselves to being a winner.

As spring training neared, some of us were actually anxious for it to begin. We figure that anything would be better than Medina. Some of us figured wrong.

Gary Shaw today

The young Gary Shaw

The author as a high-school star

Gary Shaw at Texas

Chachie Owens—at Texas and today

Darrell "Daddy D" Royal

Gene Bledsoe

Frank Erwin

Frank Medina

Lan Hewlett

Spring Training

Running a football team is no different from running any other kind of organization—an army, a political party, a business. The problems are the same. The objective is to win.

—Vince Lombardi

That we pursue something passionately does not always mean that we really want it or have a special aptitude for it. Often, the thing we pursue most passionately is but a substitute for the one thing we really want and cannot have. It is usually safe to predict that the fulfillment of an excessively cherished desire is not likely to still our nagging anxiety.

—Eric Hoffer

Wesley Barnes had the attitude every coach wants. Wesley received one of the few battlefield promotions I ever saw at Texas.

On Monday midway through our freshman season, Culpepper took the orange shirt symbolic of first team off a much bigger, better athlete named Bob Stanley and turning to Barnes announced: "Little man, I'm making you first team. That's the kind of effort I want out there." Then turning to us, "Men, if the rest of you wanted it half as bad as Wesley Barnes, we'd be unbeatable."

Wesley had talked all fall of becoming starting linebacker for the University of Texas. As he pulled on the orange jersey, his smile reflected his pride. All five feet ten, 180 pounds of him beamed. "I made it! I did it! I made it!" The rest of us looked down at the ground embarrassed at his lack of control.

Wesley had obviously been recruited for the same reason that he had made first team All-State at Corpus Christi High School: desire. If directed, he would have charged Memorial Stadium, and without blinking, collided with the concrete tiers that supported Texas football. He was continually sticking his head into anything that moved on the field. In fact, he spoke proudly of the several concussions that had resulted from this habit, including one that first fall. Wesley had only one serious drawback: his body. He wasn't fast and he didn't look as if he was going to grow. Wesley then compounded the problem by tearing two cartilages in his left knee. Three weeks before the first day of spring training, he was still on crutches. And with less than a week to go, this left knee would completely give out from under him when he tried to run.

"My knee was really hurting. I tried to go on it, but it just wouldn't hold up." This was complicated by the fact that Wesley kept having an allergic reaction to his stitches.

Then only a couple of days before spring workouts were to begin, Wesley saw the team surgeon, Dr. Buckley.

"He told me that he'd put it to me straight. He said that Coach Royal thought I looked well enough to play, and he knew that Royal didn't like guys who wouldn't get out and play when they were hurt.

"So I tried to run on it again, but it was no better. Finally I went to see Coach Pittman. He told me to see Frank and do what he said. Frank looked it over and said that I couldn't play on it. He told me to put it in the whirlpool and keep it wrapped."

Wesley was in sweats with this knee still wrapped fifteen minutes before we were to go on the field for our first spring workout. I was preparing to speak to Wesley when Coach Mike Campbell's words (he was the head defensive coordinator) came between us. "Barnes, what are you doing in sweats?" Wesley flashed a sheepish grin that said, "Ah c'mon, coach, you know I'm hurt."

Without hesitation, Campbell ordered, "get dressed."

Wesley's face then fell into shock and with his lips still upturned imitating a smile, he mumbled, "Coach, I can't even run on it."

"Barnes, as of right now, you are officially cured—get your gear on."

I peered down at the concrete floor, pretending I hadn't heard, and turned to put on my helmet. Wesley said nothing.

During the next week, the coaches would use Wesley as a ball carrier in the linebackers' tackling drill. This meant

he would be the only ball carrier for thirty, forty-five minutes running against Tommy Nobis and the other linebackers.

"There was no doubt in my mind what they were trying
to do," he told me.

Coach Campbell knew Wesley's body would never measure up to Longhorn quality, and Texas simply wasn't going
to waste time on "bad meat." Medina placed a metal brace
on this left knee and Barnes began with the rest of us.

When fresh, locker rooms usually have the scent of an
old working companion. However, the first day of spring
training, I recognized an odor that I knew in the eighth
grade, during the opening days of workouts all through
high school, and those first long days at Texas. It was the
sweat of nervous male bodies unwillingly crowded together
with the staid perfume of footpowder, sticky tasteless tape,
and stale wool socks making futile efforts to overpower
that non-masculine smell. A somber, Spartan horseplay
was the prevailing mood. It was similar to a pre-game
atmosphere, but without the excited feeling of possible
victory. Most of us seemed to be preparing to embark on
some dangerous and undesirable mission, but were resigned
to its necessity.

I felt it was a personal test that everyone must go through
and was busy assuring myself with variations of a basic
speech I always gave my body. "I can do it, just like the
others. I was scared before our first contact started in the
fall and I started on the freshman team, didn't I? All I
could do is my best: anyway, in three hours it will be
over." As always, these thoughts helped batter my anxiety
into submission, leaving my body numb.

Going out onto the practice field for spring training was
much more difficult than for a game. When the gates

opened up before a game, we would burst onto the field
in one yelling mass, and our adrenalin gave us the jolt
necessary to turn our purpose into violence and rage for
the enemy. But going onto the practice field this first day
of spring training, we walked individually, moving with
controlled fear. Those of us who seemed most restrained
scored higher than the rest. So I forced my body to move
deliberately and casually, although this allowed the anxiety
and dread to take a firmer grip.

"Now men, it's going to be hot and tough and you're
going to be tired and sore—but right now during the
spring is where we find out who our hitters are, who really
wants to play," said Daddy D in the tone of a stern seer
who knew our predestined fate.

While he spoke we all tried to appear eager and alert,
simulating purpose in our eyes in place of the missing
enthusiasm. As the sun came down on our faces, while
we were still digesting bits of resignation, a shrill whistle
violently snapped this mood in two. Our nerves jumped
and clamored even before we moved. We jogged to the
beginning calisthenics, hollering and banging our hands—
our guts derided the sham. Three hours later, our tired
aching bodies would clap themselves in genuine glee as
we strode toward the showers. Something seems inherently
wrong when a game meant for fun is played only through
external motivation. Even Royal, who makes sounds about
the fun and love we players have for the game, knows the
truth and occasionally speaks it.

"At Texas we don't encourage comedians. I don't want
comic relief to get out of control. I don't discourage jokes
or keep boys throttled down if there's something they want
to say, but I don't want the situation to get to an informal
point where they're running up and giving me a hotfoot.

Like every other squad, we have some silly little traditions,
like nicknames or a little applause routine. If somebody
busts a signal or goofs, a player will yell, 'How about three
for old Fred?' And the squad will clap three times. Just
something to keep it from being too grim. But the only
way I know how to keep football fun is to win. That's
the only answer. There is no laughter in losing." [1]

Or again speaking of the inherent love of the game that
college football encourages Royal says, "Now if you want
to see an emotionless game, you take away that band and
the twirlers and the cheering sections. You take away that
newspaper coverage and the television and radio. Take
away the crowds and put two teams together on a vacant
lot and tell them to have at it. You'll see the darndest mess
of pushing and pulling and a complete absence of people
pursuing and whacking each other. It would be duller than
an amateur wrestling match between King Farouk and
Elsa Maxwell. It's the fanfare and hoopla and the batons
and drums and headlines that prompt these real go-get 'em
efforts." [2] And on this first day of spring training there was
no band, no fans . . . and no fun.

Those who actually love the game itself should mourn
its loss. I don't think there is anything inherently anti-fun
in the raw form of the game, but in its current setting, fun
is practically impossible. Sure there is the excitement of a
game, with all the hoopla and satisfaction of victory, but
where is the love and joy of the game itself? When I was
a small kid we used to play ball—all kinds, day after day,
with no adults around, no trophies, no fans, no bands, and
no external pressure—and we loved it. Maybe football

---

[1] *Darrell Royal Talks Football*, p. 176
[2] Ibid.

could again become a pleasure, a game where a kid could express and create himself, rather than a Kafka *Trial*.

Every spring afternoon our biggest moment was posted on a tack board in the locker room. It had the same information as the tack board in Daddy D's office. This tack board had a piece of paper that listed our positions and team rankings, and was the first thing we saw walking in the door. There were always several players crowded around tensely peering over a shoulder to see their fate. It was changed daily and the top read from left end to right end, with the backfield in the lower half of the page. We started off with seven or eight teams. Those of us most anxious were third- and fourth-teamers—a couple of slips and we were in shit drills. (Shit drillers were usually all those below the fourth team.)

There were two disastrous signals carried on this eight-inch-long chart. One was dropping down several teams or below the fourth. From second to third was serious; but something like first to fourth was disastrous. It probably meant some radical reappraisal had been made. Of course, in the long run it often turned out that many of these sudden drops were only to motivate a player. The other disaster was a radical change in position. For instance, if you were a quarterback and were moved to guard, no one had to tell you what it meant. A slight position change from left tackle to right tackle didn't necessarily mean anything. Throughout spring training these team standings fluctuated almost daily. It was all we thought about on the way to the field house.

However, at the end of the first week, I was actually becoming moderately comfortable with the chart since it had listed me second-team left guard almost from the start. But on the day of our seventh workout, I looked at the

second-team left guard slot, and it read LANDRY instead of
SHAW. "Oh, my God—where is it? Nowhere in the left
guards—maybe I'm second-team somewhere else." A quick
glance at left tackle produced nothing . . . center . . .
right guard . . . first . . . second . . . third . . . Shit!
Fourth-team right guard! I quickly looked to see who was
standing around me—"I hope they don't see it." The first
topic of conversation was always "Where are you running
today?" If the answer was mumbled, you knew it was below the third team. I walked off in a daze—bumping into
anyone coming the opposite direction from my now-distant
locker. What did I do wrong yesterday? I thought I had a
good workout. Are they down on me? Is this the beginning
step toward shit drills? Not only dropped me two places,
but I changed positions. God, today is Wednesday—we're
having a goal-line scrimmage. I hope I just get in—today
is it—it's got to be all out. The following night and day of
my drop from second to fourth, a single tape rolled in my
mind. Even through all my classes, my entire world was
centered on "What team will I be on today?" And throughout the rest of spring, this chart was to occupy a large part
of my thoughts.

These position changes were very seldom discussed with
us personally. Reasons were not given and it was understood that they were to be accepted without question. Yet
they were so rapid and seemingly unpredictable that some
players finally developed a stoic attitude toward the chart.
However, I never did.

Then midway through the spring I was hurt (blood clotting on my arm) and missed all the remaining workouts.
In two weeks my whole world had disintegrated. Not only
was I not a star, I wasn't even called by name (we got that
at least on the freshman team). If my name hadn't been

on the chart each day before workouts, I would have sworn that the coaches didn't even know my position. No coach seemed aware of my existence or injury. Only once did I hear Royal mention my name. This was to Frank Medina the trainer when he asked him if the clotting would be gone in time for the final spring game. (I happened to be there and overheard this.)

My father would call and ask how Royal and the coaches thought I'd been doing—what they had said to me. He figured I'd be redshirted, but he thought it would be great if I could be a sophomore starter. I didn't know what to say to him when he'd ask what they'd said to me. They hadn't said anything, but I couldn't tell him that. I remember thinking that they must have found out that I was different or that I didn't like to hit that much, and at any time they would ask me to leave. I began to believe that the only thing that had saved me from shit drills was my injury, and finally, toward the end of spring training, I started imagining that the coaches were purposely avoiding me. In just two weeks, it seemed I had dropped from high school hero and freshman big shot to nonentity.

"Spring practice is pretty much drudgery no matter how much camouflage you stack around it. But we try to preach this to the squad: Spring practice is competitive, just as the Saturday games in the Fall. I tell the players that this very afternoon, over in College Station, the Aggies are going through a Spring drill and they're just as tired and sore as we are. Up at Waco, Baylor is doing the same thing. Everybody is wishing this Spring practice would hurry and finish." [3] However, there is no hurry to finish on the part of the coaching staff. Although only twenty official

---

[3] Ibid.

workouts are allowed, these are usually stretched from the first week in March to the middle of April. This is to maximize the hitting and usefulness of each workout. In between these nicely spaced spring days are films, blackboard instruction, physical recovery, and more films. These days come in the middle of the spring semester and occupy half of it. This is the time for the coaches to find their most dedicated players. To fall in that category means no eating, sleeping, or bathroom visits without football occupying all voluntary parts of the mind.

Obviously, many sources of desire were needed for pumping enthusiasm into this organized, mechanical drudgery. As Royal put it: "What has brought about this biggest change in college football, this dedicated pursuit? Film study, for one thing. The concentrated study of game movies has made coaches and players more conscious of all-out effort and aggressiveness on every play. A player's moves on every step of every play are a matter of celluloid record. He realizes this fact. If he's a proud lad, he doesn't want his coaches studying the game film and seeing him loaf on any play. Subconsciously, perhaps, he wants to go on record as a Bearcat."

And during the spring there were filmed scrimmages at least every Wednesday and Saturday. The minutes prior to one of these films provided a unique kind of tenseness. We were like kids called to the principal's office and not knowing exactly why. Simultaneously, we tried to be pleasant enough to win favor and let the coaches know we were on their side; while at the same time, we were already apologetic, anticipating some reprimand. There was always some self-

---

[4] Ibid.

conscious teasing of one another and reserved attempts at light conversation with the coaches. Usually our performances had fallen enough in the middle range that none of us knew what to expect. The coaches were masters at getting the most mileage from this atmosphere. For example, during the films one small comfort was the darkness of the room which made it hard to see one another. But occasionally after running someone's mistake over and over, the film projector would stop and the lights would come on. Then, with all attention on the guilty player, the coaches would continue their derisive comments. Like older brothers, the rest of us would self-righteously turn and stare at the pale face of our fallen comrade.

After the films and position chart, probably the most important part of our tangible world was the football field. A football field can have a ritual importance of its own. In high school, it was common for many of us to walk over the stadium turf a few hours before game time. If it was a home game, I always spent at least thirty minutes walking over and around Bronco field. It was a tie to some solid support—as if in the fourth quarter there would at least be familiar turf that connected that moment to some other previously passed test. The field was a comrade that had seen us spill blood and effort and certainly would not abandon us in the big trial of a game. At times during a game there was something almost pleasant about being bashed to a familiar ground. It was as if I was as close to the earth as possible and could not be pushed deeper—it was the end of my fall and a source of memory that could be counted on. Before a game in another team's stadium, our coaches would tell us to go out and get a feel of the turf. I think that this practice was unconsciously much more than to familiarize ourselves with where we would be playing. In fact, it seems similar to common war rituals where the participants carry souvenirs from the location or terrain of one battle into another. On entering a battle, the warriors know that some of them will die, and I think there is an effort to hold on to and identify with something that will endure even after death. By tying themselves to an object that is also in some way involved in the battle, they can cling to a seemingly indestructible part of themselves. Of course, a football game is not such a dramatic life-or-death situation, but I think it represents a great deal of symbolic threat. We knew that not only would there be physical pain, but we could get seriously hurt. More importantly, we could possibly be defeated without really hitting—devastated and wiped out by fear. Every time we took to that field there was a chance that this fear of hitting or some lack of desire would overpower us, and because our identities were so immersed in being a football player who is unafraid to hit, this was frightening and immensely threatening. So anything that we could tie ourselves to and identify with in these battles provided at least some security. The field was the most likely candidate. It was one constant in the high-anxiety situations of a game, and our bodies had already had intimate contact with it. Everytime we played a game, it was there. So in some vague way we were part of the turf. Even with our own blood and injury, or some sort of symbolic destruction of our male identity, the turf would still leave us something known and tangible.

In a somewhat different way, the Texas practice field seemed to have a football personality of its own. It was plainly flat and surrounded by higher terrain on all sides. On one side were rich green trees and a clear gentle creek.

On another was a dormitory that stretched high above the east corner. Looking up toward this dorm we could see the curious watching from their windows as well as students sunbathing on the adjoining hill. Right next to the creek and particularly visible in the southwest corner was always busy San Jacinto Street, and in its background the state capitol. On the north side was a fence that separated the practice field from a fifteen-foot incline that housed a school parking lot. Between this parking lot and the dorm, if we looked just right, we could see the campus tower and hear its chimes. Sitting in the middle of all this with, coincidentally enough, an oval shape, was our rather dull, colorless field. Its ground was hard and most of its grass had been chewed up by metal cleats. Being somewhat in a pit with a creek next to it, it had the most humid breath in Austin. One might think that such a dreary place would be engulfed by all the life around it. Quite the contrary, it seemed as if it had purposely placed all this superior scenery around us. In this way it would be much easier to remind us of its homely strength. "The life I promise you is hard and Spartan, but deny yourself for me and I will reward you with much more than you see around you. You can look and be tempted, but you are mine." And indeed, something about just working out on that field gave me illusions of strength from the power of denial. It also had a way of stretching itself out and seemed to encompass much more earth than it actually did.

As any coach will tell you, "The more you leave on that practice field, the more important it becomes to win." And that practice field was talking to us each day when it surrounded us with the beauty of an Austin spring. Its deep setting told us that we were apart—somehow different from the rest. Others couldn't subsist on getting life and blood from its hard belly. And indeed one could tell the less dedicated by the number of times they looked up to see the tower clock. Those more disciplined were able to avoid all but an occasional furtive glance.

However, the main way of avoiding these furtive glances and keeping our enthusiasm high was to make the spring a constant series of daily tests. This was done by repeatedly putting our male egos against each other—hitting. Each drill of every day there was hitting . . . and more hitting. Injuries didn't have to be worried about as there would be no games for six months. What better way of testing our dedication.

Everyone had enough psyche to hit for a while, but the true test was who could continue to do it day after day. The last two springs at Texas I did well and started in our final intra-squad games. I always came up in team standing the second half of spring training as others fell by the wayside. I think my "secret" was an ability to numb myself. I would gradually come not to notice my bruises, soreness, and body pain. "Men, you must toughen yourself against feeling body pain and soreness." Contact came to have a strange, distant feel to it. It must be similar to the numbness a boxer has when being pulverized. By my second spring at Texas, I would even catch myself looking at one of my sore and painful ankles in disgust, while I mumbled, "Goddamn ankle"—said as if I were talking to some out-of-favor possession. Perhaps I would touch it with sympathy as if an old favorite, but as a possession nonetheless.

So to be successful meant to wear pain and injury as some merit badge. I think this ability to dissociate from your own body is the key to those able to endure the most pain. And I think that the bulking up football players do is at least partly to further dissociate themselves from body feeling—to put more padding between the point of contact and the soul. Thus, those most integrated with their body feeling were those least likely to succeed.

This ceaseless hitting and competition, with the serious consequences of failing, made for uneasy friendships and increasing isolation. Since we believed that the "winning-losing" distinction separated men from "others," we were put in a very uncomfortable bind. To be a winner meant to make some of our friends losers. But it was hard to escape guilt, as some small part of us must have realized that we were cooperating in defining our teammates as shits. It was not just a matter of competition leading to some of us playing and others not. In fact, by defeating our teammates, we were helping to eliminate them by putting them in shit drills or some other untenable position. Anytime other players were treated with a total lack of concern, we had to justify this by either ignoring it or accepting the idea that our friends were losers. It was nearly impossible to accept this belief system of the coaches and still keep friendships with these losers. Yet there was also some belief in the loyalty of friendship. But predictably, this inconsistency and conflict led to most increasing their fanaticism and belief in the system. So the circle of winners would tighten in a mutual exclusion, and those that made it usually slowly separated their distance from the rest and developed what might be called "studitis." For them to believe in this system of male winners made it practically impossible not to think of themselves as "studs." By definition they were superior—real men. But to keep their delicate balloon inflated required a constant pump. All the feelings and experiences that had to be denied meant that those studs had to grab anything that would hold up this male superiority—championships, trophies, newspaper clippings, girls. Those on the first couple of teams usually socialized only with each other and even sat with one another in the dining hall. The closer players got to the top, the tougher they would act. You could almost tell a first-teamer by the open-armed swagger and coarseness of his walk that said, "I am a man."

But, once we reached this top level we were left more dependent than ever on the coach's judgment. It is a false premise that a player can affirm real power and strength simply by defeating other players. Our strength could be sent crashing at any time by a single utterance from the coaches. Frank Gifford, who reached the very top in football as the NFL's most valuable player in 1957, epitomizes this lack of real inner strength, as he speaks of Vince Lombardi.

"I came back in 1957, the most valuable player in the League, and I saw the crop of rookies coming in and I was positive some guy was going to take away my job. Call it insecurity or anything you want, but that's what I was like. That's what drove me. And Vinny [Lombardi] could put his finger on these elements in a personality. He knew exactly how to motivate. He knew just what buttons to push. You see, I didn't hide anything from him. I was always just as open as I could be with him, because I liked him so much. I know that after a while it got to the point where I was playing football for just one reason: I was always trying to please him." [5]

---

[5] Lombardi, *Winning Is the Only Thing*, p. 57.

Once the coaches had established the clear feeling of distinction between the winners and losers amongst us, it was easy enough to transfer this elite group's needs to defeating common opponents.

Gene Bledsoe

Gene Bledsoe looks like the guy Hercules always fights in his final dramatic scene. And he would certainly fall into the group of elite "winners." He was a three-year starter at Texas, all Southwest Conference two of those years, honorable mention All-American, and then a member of the New York Jets for two more years.

"Football made me feel like I was something special—without it I would have been nothing. I will be forever indebted to football and my coaches."

"What would you have done if you hadn't played football?"

"I don't even like to think about it. When I was a kid in junior high I was fat and ugly and I spent most of my time alone. My parents both worked days and went to school at nights. I didn't feel part of any group at school, I felt left out. Then football came along and it was a propulsion point, it gave me a start."

"When I was a senior in high school I was well known for football, and I think I was confident as a person; but as a freshman at Texas, the whole process started over again. I felt I had to make it in football."

"What have your coaches taught you?"

"How to be a good football player and to have more of the qualities that make for a good football player."

"What are those?"

"Courage and fortitude and learning to take it. I learned that there is no punishment that I couldn't take for thirty minutes—I could take anything.

"And I think the people who are highly successful in

business are people who, given the physical qualities, would have been successful in football. I think to be successful in anything you have to make yourself do things you don't want to do. One of the things the coaches taught me was that I could run more wind sprints than I thought I could, and punish myself more than I knew.

"And the way Coach Royal acted toward us was no different than how any other successful business executive would act."

"How would you have been affected if you hadn't made it at Texas?"

"I don't know, I can't answer that."

"Well, how were you affected when you were cut by the Jets?"

"When. . . . That's too close to the present [1969]. It affected me quite a bit, and I don't think I can talk about it yet."

Later Gene said about leaving the Jets: "There was a lot of embarrassment in facing my friends at home. But I had past football experiences to soften the shock as far as friends go."

"Do you regret not playing now?"

"No, not at all. That's so much shit to go through. I liked all the rewards you got from it, but I don't think I could push myself that much now."

"Did you ever like practice?"

"Shit no! I don't know anybody that ever did—you'd have to be kinda weird. I just like the fact of knowing that I went through it and succeeded like I did.

"And it's still important for me for people to know that I played or that I'm a program computer analyst. It gives me confidence in a crowd for someone to point out that I played football. Still the biggest thrill I get is for some old ladies to hear my name and then mention that they'd heard that name somewhere before."

"How important to you was what the Texas coaches felt about you?"

"I really used to feel great when Coach Zapalac would have me demonstrate how to block.

"I would have really felt bad if they would have thought I wasn't any good. I admired some of the guys that really tried, yet weren't any good—but I sure wouldn't have wanted to be in their shoes. I would have really felt bad if they were trying to run me off, but that would have been better than if they had totally ignored me."

"How much contact did you have with the coaches, specifically Coach Royal, outside of coaching instruction?"

Long pause. . . . "There wasn't any that I can remember. Royal was always more of an administrator. The others did the more technical coaching."

"Did you like Royal?"

"Yes."

"Why?"

"Because he was honest."

"What do you mean?"

"Well, he was fair about evaluation of who played; he didn't play favorites."

"Anything else?"

"Well, I didn't know him that well—mainly he was honest. He was the only coach who didn't promise me that I'd start at their school—even SMU promised me things."

"What things?"

"They promised me a big job with a Dallas bank when I graduated."

"Who's they?"

"A bunch of SMU ex'es that were businessmen in Dallas. They met a lot of us [recruits] in a building on the SMU campus. They told us that they all stuck together, and that they would take care of us when we got through with football. Most of the schools I went to made similar overtures. I told Royal about this when I was visiting Texas, and he told me that businesses weren't going to do something for me without expecting some contribution from me to their company. His logic in pointing this out impressed me a whole lot. This, probably more than anything else, was the reason I went to Texas."

"Do you think Royal cared about you?"

"Yes."

"Would he have still liked you if you hadn't been a starter and been on the fourth team?"

"Well, that's hard to say . . . you mean if I had the same abilities and was just—ah—lazy?"

"Yes."

"No, I don't think so. But I always went with the program and was regimented and didn't try to assert myself over the team or cause any trouble."

"It seems to me, then, that his 'liking' you was based almost entirely on your performance?"

"No, I think if I had been a good player and say . . . had been conceited, he wouldn't have liked me.

"Yow, I think Royal cared about his players. I remember after I graduated and was going to play in a post-season all-star game he let me take my own cleats, my own shoulder pads—which I had fixed just like I wanted, and my own helmet. He didn't have to do that."

"Why then do you think Royal allowed shit drills to take place?"

"Well . . . I think maybe he thought it might make

a few of them better football players. I think the coaches hoped to get some football players out of the shit squad—even though they [the coaches] had probably written about ninety percent off. However, they didn't know which of the ten percent might help the team."

"What about the ninety percent?"

"Well, he had to weed some of the weaker ones out. He had to look out for his own interests . . . and he needed their scholarships."

Shit Drills

Let us treat the men and women as if they were real—
perhaps they are.

—Emerson

In Spring training my sophomore year, I broke my neck—
four vertebrae. 'Hey, Coach,' I said, 'my neck don't feel
good.' 'There's nothing wrong with your neck, you jack-
ass,' he said. So the numb went away a little, and I made
a tackle. When I went to get up, my body got up but my
head just stayed there, right on the ground. The coach
says, 'Hey, get this jackass off the field.' So the trainer put
some ice on my neck and after practice they took me up to
the infirmary for an X-ray. The doctor said, 'Son, your
neck is broken. You got here ten minutes later, you'd be
dead.' Dead! Man, that scared me. I mean those colleges
let you lie right out there on the field and die. That's some-
thing to think about.

—Charley Taylor of the Washington Redskins
recounting his college days at Arizona State

The health and safety of our players are always utmost in
our mind.

—Darrell Royal

"What's happened to yesterday's high school football hero? Is he a hoss of the highest degree in the Southwest Conference today?

"Maybe, but don't make any wagers that he is. If you insist on a bet, come to us. We will pull the money out of your hand after flashing a few facts before your eyes.

"At great expense (five cups of coffee during the research period) we offer the following note: Of 432 high school players recruited by SWC schools in 1963 only 131 will touch a football field this fall. Even with our C-minus background in arithmetic that comes out as a sixty-two percent dropout figure. (For Texas 75 percent dropout rate)

"You can't say though that sixty-two percent of the recruits were duds. Some of the youngsters who signed letters in 1963 never made it to their chosen SWC schools. A few decided to go elsewhere at the last moment. Maybe they were injured and couldn't play. Maybe they struck out with the books. Maybe some saw they didn't have a chance to play and decided to just concentrate on their studies. And maybe, just maybe, a few took some well-placed hints and departed." [1]

An integral part of spring training was "shit drills." These drills were for the purpose of running guys off— making them quit. However, they were not just to force some of us to give up football; they were designed to be

---

[1] Bob Galt, Dallas *Times Herald*, August, 1966.

part of an experience so devastating that we would be
"persuaded" to sign away our scholarships. Now Coach
Royal and his assistants weren't crude enough to be doing
this simply for the sadistic pleasure in it. There was a practical reason. The conference rule was that at any one time
a school could have only the money equivalent of a hundred full scholarships. This, in effect, meant that no more
than one hundred boys could be on a full football scholarship at one time. The limit could be exceeded by a couple,
but anywhere close to ten percent over the conference was
to take action.

Here's an example of how this worked. If one of us
dropped out of school or otherwise gave up his scholarship
after three months, then that player would have gotten
money for only three months—and that three months
would be all that was counted against Royal's scholarship
allotment. In other words, this would be only about a third
of a scholarship based on nine months. So the limit that
couldn't be exceeded was the total money allotment which
was equal to one hundred boys being on full scholarship.
Technically each one of us could keep our scholarships
and not even show up for the first workout, and this would
still count as a full scholarship and would take one-hun-
dredth of all the total money.

From 1961 to 1964, Texas gave two hundred and seven
full scholarships.[2] Since Royal could legally have only
a hundred on scholarships, over half this two hundred plus
had to give up their scholarships for Royal to stay inside
the conference limit. Yet according to the official handbook of the Southwest Athletic Conference, "An athletic

---

[2] Compiled from 1961-1964 issues of *Texas Football*.

scholarship or other aid may not be cancelled or modified during the period of its award: (a) on the basis of a student-athlete's prowess or his contribution to a team's success; (b) because of an injury which prevents the recipient from participation in athletics; (or (c) for any other athletic reason, except such scholarship or aid may be cancelled or modified if the recipient (1) voluntarily renders himself ineligible for intercollegiate competition, or (2) fraudulently misrepresents any information on his application, letter of intent or tender, or engages in serious misconduct warranting substantial disciplinary penalty. "Serious misconduct" means conduct of sufficient gravity that if comparable conduct occurred in other departments of the institution, a similar substantial disciplinary penalty could properly be imposed. And, an "athletic scholarship, during the period of its award, may not be reduced or cancelled for disciplinary reasons, except by the committee of the institution appointed to handle disciplinary problems for all students."

Thus, it was nearly impossible for Coach Royal to simply take away our scholarships. But the more boys he had to pick from the more likely he was to have a winner. So the big problem for Royal was to get enough of us to give up our scholarships—"voluntarily" render ourselves ineligible. But how do you convince over a hundred boys to give up several thousand dollars of education that they'd been promised? And add to this the fact that the basic building block of your program is "never to quit." Obviously, some drastic was needed. It was supplied.

[An SWC rule change in 1966 eliminated the 100 full scholarships limit. Instead a yearly limit of 50 was imposed which meant it was legal to have up to 200 players on scholarship at any one time. The need for shit drills was greatly reduced and the retention rate of the next year's (1967) SWC recruits almost doubled the 1963 and 1964 rate. Some 60.5 per cent of the 1967 stayed for four years (63 per cent at Texas).[3]]

However, recently the SWC reinstituted a full scholarship limit—this time at 130. It will be interesting to see if the retention rates suddenly begin dropping again.

After four or five days of spring training, our freshman year, approximately forty-five players were instructed to follow Pat Culpepper to the northeast corner of the practice field—an area within a few yards of the creek. These shit drillers were farther away from the rest of us than other drills; but more importantly they were surrounded by a psychological wall that separated them from the rest of us. These forty-five were all scholarship players who happened to be below the fourth team. There was no division according to interior linemen, ends or backs, and for these forty-five, there was only one coach—Culpepper. While the rest of us went from one area of the field to another with different drills and coaches, these forty-five stayed in their one corner repeating the same few drills over and over.

To the untrained eye some of these drills might seem of no different nature from any other. And of course, the coaches would publicly claim that they were simply for the purpose of practicing fundamentals. But we all knew the difference—especially the players participating in them. Part of the differences were physical, part psychological. There were only a few of these drills, so I'll diagram them. They began with this drill:

---

[3] Figures from an article by Bob Galt, Dallas *Times Herald,* Summer 1970.

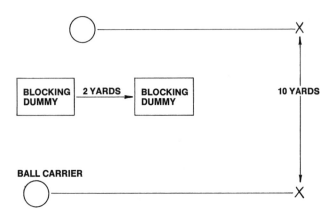

Two players lined up ten yards apart, facing each other
between two blocking dummies. One was to be the ball-
carrier, the other the tackler. They were to run to point X,
turn ninety degrees up the field, and then go full speed
toward one another. It doesn't sound so bad until you consider a few of the unique factors in this drill. For one,
there was no discrimination as to who carried the ball.
Linemen carried it just as often as backs. Apparently, one
of the fundamentals the coaches were interested in developing was the ball-carrying ability of the guards and
tackles. And as any running back knows, it is an acquired
knowledge to learn to protect yourself while carrying the
ball. Another unusual characteristic of this drill was that
there was no tackling; the two were to meet full speed
ahead—helmet to helmet—two bulls butting heads. Also
in this drill, as in the others, it seemed that the boys just
never could quite do anything right, and there was, shall
we say, a frequent amount of immediate repetition.

   In another drill five players were able to participate at
the same time. The one in the middle held a football and
was called the ball carrier. Four men surrounded him, each
at a distance of fifteen yards. Each of these four was given

a number, one through four. Culpepper would call out one of the numbers and whoever had that number was to head with "reckless abandon" at the ball carrier who could not move except in a stationary jog. The "numbered" player was to tackle the ball carrier.

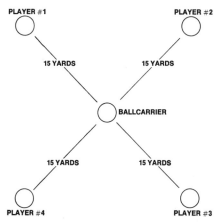

But again there were a few original added attractions. One was that Culpepper would quite frequently become a bit confused in his timing and call out two, three, even four numbers consecutively, without a pause. This meant that one of the four would still be several yards from the ball carrier when another tackler's number was called. This second tackler was not to wait for the ball carrier and first tackler to get off the ground. He was to drill directly into them, and if a third or fourth was right behind, they were all to meet in this mass centered on the ball carrier. Naturally, the ballcarrier was usually tackled again while still on the ground. Worse yet, he would be about halfway up in getting to his feet when cracked from behind, or neatly sandwiched by two players arriving simultaneously. This drill did not serve to just toughen the ball carrier, it also worked for the tacklers. This was due to the fact that their bodies often traveled to the center at the same time, which made for quite a tangle of bodies. This drill was rather cynically referred to by Culpepper as "broken-field running."

The third drill was the fifteen-yard sideline drill, and was first developed for Tommy Cade and Chachie Owens, who were proving somewhat resistant to getting their fundamentals down.

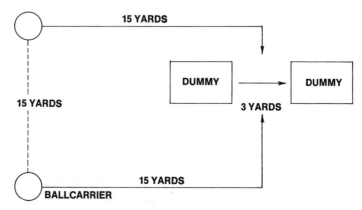

Here there were two players fifteen yards apart, one with the ball and one without. They were to run fifteen yards and then turn upfield, and while running as fast as they could, meet between the dummies with their heads. Now heading full speed straight at someone from fifteen yards apart rarely happens in a football game, and when it does, as perhaps on a kickoff, someone is often shaken up or hurt. As anyone connected with football will tell you, if you do this enough times, someone will get hurt. This is especially true if a player has gone repeatedly when his body is aching and tired. Under these circumstances it is much more difficult for him to be able to protect himself. These head-on collisions at such distance are most likely to occur on kickoffs, which is why they have special teams in pro football called "suicide squads." And even on those kickoffs, the ball carrier and tackler are usually not both going full speed at the point of the tackle. Even if they are, the tackle is generally made at some kind of angle, not head-on. In addition, the men involved in those kickoffs are usually fresh and rested, making it less likely they'll get hurt. Besides, the pros realize the great risk factor in this type of collision, and don't even practice kickoff tackling during the week. But these drills went on for two and a half hours a day. And as Chachie, who was one of the forty-five, said, "Most were literally killed off. They would pit us in a way to most quickly eliminate people. For a long time I went against John Jolly who was five feet six and 210 pounds. I killed Jolly off, but Jolly killed off lots of others. Our punishment was injuries."

Coordinated with all the physical abuse were the psychological factors. The rest of us could hear Culpepper all over the field: "You guys are the sorriest excuses for football players I've seen." Here is an example which I observed and was typical. The chief assistant coach for Orange Hill School—Chachie's high school—came to workouts to see Chachie. He was introduced to the coaches and was brought over to the shit drills. When Chachie's next turn came, Culpepper said, "All right, Charles O-w-e-n-s"—dragging his last name out for emphasis— "let's see you hit someone for a change." After contact was made, Culpepper went into an animated rage. "We're going to make a football player out of you or run you off. Do it again." And after the second time: "Charles Owens, you're the sorriest excuse for a football player I've ever seen. Get out of my sight—go back to the end of the line." The entire time Chachie's high school coach was not more than fifteen feet away.

"The whole time Culpepper knew I was injured and

hadn't been able to hit anyone for three days, and that I'd
be embarrassed in front of my old coach."

Chachie's injuries at the time were one badly separated
shoulder and one that was severely bruised and slightly
separated. But he was not allowed to go to the doctor since
it was Medina who decided if the injury was serious
enough to see a physician. After spring training Chachie
went to a hometown doctor who verified these injuries.

In a fourth drill there were again two players approximately fifteen to twenty yards apart. Both were to run full
tilt toward point X twenty yards away. Culpepper was
standing twenty yards from point X and had a football.
Just before they both reached this point, he would throw
the football to the one marked runner.

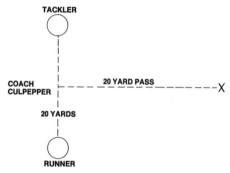

The idea was that just as the runner was reaching up
to catch the football the tackler would hit him. Of course,
reaching up for the pass would leave the runner unpro-
tected. If a pass receiver gets hurt it's usually on this type
of contact, they dread it more than any other kind of contact. And again, part of the fundamentals the coaches
seemed interested in developing was having guards and
tackles learning how to catch a pass while being tackled.

What effect did these drills have on their participants?

"The psychological impact was knowing that you were

big enough to kill off these guys, but also realizing that daily you were coming apart physically so that one day soon you would be so weakened that you would get yours. It was knowing that there was no chance of survival, yet your pride wouldn't let you quit. We soon realized that there was no interest in our athletic ability, and we stopped killing each other off and began to 'brother-in-law.' We were determined to beat them [coaches] at their own game if we accomplished nothing else. This led them to devise the all-against-one drill." [4]

Most of these drills, at least superficially, could be explained possibly by Coach Royal in a way to convince one that they were simply for the development of fundamentals. But one drill—the all-against-one or euphemistically called "the Sideline Drill" by Culpepper—would give even Royal's persuasive powers extreme difficulty.

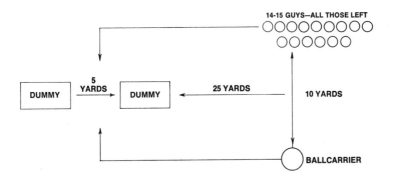

---

[4] Chachie Owens recounting the effects he felt.

At this point there were only fifteen of the original forty-five left, and these fifteen had obviously learned to beat the coaches at their own game, to be still surviving. So for them it was going to take something a little cruder. This drill was it. One ball carrier stood ten yards away from all the rest. To make sure everyone got up enough momentum, they were to run twenty-five yards before turning upfield. All were to meet (at the same time) between the two dummies which were five yards apart. Fifteen en masse on one side, a lone ball carrier on the other. Chachie Owens told me what happened to him the first time he was this lone ball carrier.

"Five guys got there first and tackled me, the other ten ran over me. Someone's cleats ripped my calf open. I didn't get up fast and Culpepper came screaming for me to get up. He took one look at my open leg and gagged, then called the trainers, who slowly walked over. The doctor and I walked a block and a half to his truck, and he drove me to the health center. There it took about a hundred stitches to close my calf."

At this point one of his shoulders was already separated, the other hurt.

"Getting my leg injured saved my career at Texas. I couldn't have taken four weeks of it—no one could have."

This statement about no one being able to take four weeks of these drills is not a statement based on just his particular situation. Those drills started out with forty-five guys and ended after three weeks with just five guys left, and they weren't part of the original forty-five.

Every time I looked over at those drills, someone else was down on the ground, hurt. It was a constant reminder to put out and not fall below the fourth team.

The rest of us were very wary about being around these

shit drillers—especially when it seemed they were getting
close to quitting. I remember Rusty telling me I'd better
start avoiding Chachie because he had overheard Chachie
wondering aloud if it was all worth it. Rusty liked Chachie
but genuinely felt his suggestion of avoiding him was in
my own interest. He said that I had a bright future ahead
as a Longhorn and that being around Chachie might get
me thinking in the wrong way. Soon I sensed that Chachie
did want to quit, so I began to make up excuses why I
couldn't see him . . . and tightened my resolve to survive.
"X-ing" out my friend when he was a shit driller, depressed, and close to quitting was part of being a winner.
And while we might have been sympathetic, we were sympathetic at a safe distance.

Still I used to worry about my associating with some of
the shit drillers—I didn't want Coach Royal to think they
influenced me. Because there was the general belief among
the rest of us that most of these shit drillers were lacking
something. So if any coaches were around I'd pretend to
ignore Chachie and the rest. Yet I never remember seeing
Coach Royal watch shit drills. In fact, no coach besides
Culpepper would get near them.

Of course, the main way of getting out of these drills
was to be injured seriously enough. But with the policy of
Medina determining who saw a doctor, the injury had to
be off sufficient gravity and flagrantly obvious. Yet many,
like Chachie, were seriously enough injured anyway, so
how did the coaches keep pressure on those not physically
able to work out?

Here Royal was not lacking in imagination. He had all
injured players (if below the first few teams) wear a jersey
with a big red cross stenciled on both sides. And if at all
able to walk, the injured were to continually jog around

the practice field the complete workout. The red crosses were to be signs of humiliation. And throughout the spring, Royal would refer to the guys that would do anything to get out of workout and "couldn't take it." It may sound silly, but it was really an embarrassing stigma to be standing out there on the practice field with a big red cross on your jersey. I only missed eight spring training workouts the entire four years—all coming that first spring. But those eight I missed, I wore the jersey and red cross. Any time a player on one of the first two teams came near me, I would suddenly be occupied—ducking my head and hoping that they wouldn't notice. It was never explained to us why only those injured below a certain team were "fake injuries." There were always several members on the first few teams who were injured, yet they wore only solid jerseys.

So why didn't the players on lower teams just quit? "Every coach likes to impress on his squad that defeat is something that comes from within. Defeat must be admitted before it is a reality," Royal has said.

And if you're like most, you think you can hold out—and maybe you can for a year, even two; but that's a lot of days, a lot of Medinas, a lot of running the stands, and a lot of shit drills. And how long do you really think you can spend all your time around people who think you're shit?

"Chachie" Owens

*I'll lose that race, because I'm not a race horse at all, and
I'll let him know it . . . I'm a human being and I've got
thoughts and secrets and bloody life inside me that he
doesn't know is there . . .*

—THE LONELINESS OF THE LONG-DISTANCE RUNNER

If the University of Texas football team had anyone close to being a real rebel, it was Charles (Chachie) Owens. "I always had the sense that Royal was afraid that if I became a star and anyone even interviewed me, I might say the wrong things."

His thorough confidence seemed misplaced in our Moore-Hill world. It was too general. As football players we were expected to have very specific sorts of arrogance, especially about our football ability, but otherwise remain humble. The reasons are obvious. People like Chachie don't automatically abdicate their rights, they have a feeling of their own inner worth. And this inner worth does not need constant reinforcement by coaches.

Chachie's confidence was not prep school arrogance, nor the arrogance of someone who knows he's physically intimidating. Instead, he had almost a relaxed arrogance that lets you know that he's got everything under control.

In fact, he seemed as sure of himself as an eighteen-year-old can be, even though he had been brought up in the same "winning is everything" atmosphere as the rest of us. But the one big difference was that he began learning early that there was no proper authority for determining the rules of the game.

"My father taught me that I didn't have to take shit off anyone. When I was in high school, there was one particular instance when I got into a pretty heavy dispute with school authorities. Instead of automatically siding with them, he agreed with me, and he went straight up to the principal's office and gave them hell. He was always

136

like that. He felt that the most important thing for me to learn was to stand up for myself. He repeatedly told me that I'd have to learn to take care of myself because no one else would.

"We lived in a really tough neighborhood, you might say the wrong side of the tracks. My father had dropped out of school early and we were pretty poor. Most of our neighborhood was black. I was in a fight every other day, kicked a lot of butts, and got mine kicked a lot."

Adding to this early strain of independence was the fact that "When I was a kid I spent a lot of my time on my own. My father went back to school, worked days and went to school at night. (His father graduated with honors and has since become a very successful businessman.) So I got used to being on my own, going it alone."

The only bitter remnant of this tough upbringing is Chachie's strong tendency to distrust other peoples' motivations. "If you don't watch it, people will screw your ass." Combined with this early independent strength was the fact that by the tenth grade Chachie was connecting himself enthusiastically to a multitude of things around him.

"My parents were always encouraging me to find things to do for myself." By his senior year Chachie was a campus leader, into acting, president of his honor society and international vice-president of the Key Club as well as leading a student campaign to bring a school for the mentally retarded to his home town. He gave a speech before the Texas House of Representatives when he was seventeen.

"Football was only a part of my life. It was always just an extracurricular activity: I always thought of myself as a human being and student first. Being a jock was secondary."

Yet all this did not seem to curtail Chachie's athletic achievement. He was first team All-State as a fullback with his high school backfield being on the cover of the Texas football magazine, *Scholastic Coaches*. He was also offered a large bonus to sign a professional baseball contract. He was very widely recruited for football, and because of his grades and score on the college board exams, was offered scholarships by several Ivy League schools.

Chachie didn't look much like a football player. He's only five feet eight and played at about 210 pounds. His rounded face sat on a rounded body that topped the flattest feet I've ever seen. (They were flat enough to keep him out of the Army.) I often called him "fat boy." He'd just laugh and say, "Pass the butter." Now he sports a beard and very much resembles Peter Ustinov.

Despite this rounded appearance, women always went for Chachie. I used to wonder why until I realized that they liked him for the same reasons I did, relaxed confidence and enthusiasm, great humor and easy laughter, all spiced with a terrific imagination. He was continually into something new, always looking for the big deal. "Shaw, listen to this, I've got the greatest idea. . ." The ebullient entrepreneur. Somewhere very early in life his tough strength had mellowed into an independent sureness that had a little bit of the con-man wink in his eye.

The playfulness is exemplified by the time Chachie went to a rather large New Left political meeting on campus. He purposely sat in the back of the room until the middle of the meeting when he suddenly stood up and demanded to be heard. He then ambled to the podium and gave a long rambling speech on behalf of Richard Nixon! With tongue in cheek and not a smile on his face amidst stunned silence, he ended his ten-minute oratory with "and thank you, my fellow Americans."

Afterward, he asked me, "Shaw, did you see the look on those faces?" and continued to roar the rest of the night.

Of course, Chachie was not always unflappable. One such instance I call "Fat Boy meets Big Red." Big Red was Chachie's favorite possession. It was an alarm clock that was at least eight inches in diameter. Large metal bells were on each side with a hammer in the middle that went back and forth between the two at a rapid speed. It had big black numerals, black hands, and a white face. It looked as if someone had a put a clock in a big can, then sealed it from the back. When Big Red rang, it rang so hard that it walked along the back of the bed—sometimes even toppling off onto Chachie.

Chachie talked about Big Red as if it was a pet dog. "Well time to go to bed now. I'm going to set Big Red. . . . There's not an alarm clock anywhere I'd trade in for Big Red."

He was constantly showing everyone how loud Big Red could ring. "Man, you sure as hell don't have to worry about Big Red waking you up."

At the time, Chachie had the worst room in the dorm. (This was when they were trying to run him off.) It was the worst room for a number of reasons. It was the smallest, and a big desk sat right in the middle of the floor. No one knew what this big desk was doing in the room but it was the size of a kitchen table. In fact, this desk was so large that when Chachie pulled his bed out to sleep the bed and desk touched.

So once in bed, Chachie would have to climb out of one

end of his bed to get to the door. Even with the bed pushed in he could only walk between the bed and desk sideways.

One Saturday night when Chachie was out I paid a dorm counselor five dollars to let me into his room. Once I got in, I took Big Red off its place on the shelf—Chachie always kept it in the same place—and set it to go off at four in the morning.

There was another feature to the room that was shared by all others in Moore-Hill. This was a wood-paneled storage compartment that was under the beds. These paneled compartments were only about a foot high but opened up all the way back to the wall. Supposedly, they were for storing extra shoes and miscellany.

After setting Big Red, I placed it in this paneled compartment under the head of Chachie's bed. Then I used a baseball bat to push Big Red as far to the back as it would go.

When Chachie came in later the first thing he noticed was that Big Red was gone. "Goddamn, somebody took Big Red. I'll kill the son-of-a-bitch if I ever find out who it was!" He went all around the dorm waking up people and asking them if they'd seen Big Red. I went around with him helping him look. (I'd sworn on a blood oath I knew nothing about Big Red's disappearance.)

Finally, about three in the morning, he gave up looking and went to bed. I went to tank up on coffee and get ready for the action.

At four I was hiding outside Chachie's door when Big Red went off. Its *clang! clang!* started bouncing off those wooden panels and seemed twice as loud as ever before. In about five seconds I heard a clump followed by a moan —Chachie had jumped up so quickly he'd hit his knees against the desk.

"Goddamn it! Goddamn it! What the hell!" Still groggy, Chachie attempted to get up but his 210 pounds thudded to the floor.

"Goddamn it! Shit!"

The lights in his room went on, and Chachie shouted, "Where is that Red son-of-a-bitch." Big Red was still going *clang! clang!* That hammer was beating those bells unmercifully.

About this time a guy in a room across the hall came stumbling out.

"What's going on in there?"

Chachie came to the door cursing. "Some son-of-a-bitch put Big Red under my bed."

Finally Chachie had to get a coat hanger, squat his chubby body between that bed and desk and grab for Big Red. "I'll kill the son-of-a-bitch that did this."

Clang! Clang! Clang!

It took Chachie fifteen minutes and three coat hangers to get Big Red. I could hear him cursing the whole time and I was rolling in the hall.

When Chachie came to Texas, his need to win and make it, prove himself, was still very present. But unlike most of us, it was only a part of him and not a structure that had him completely bricked in. So, though as a freshman and sophomore he wanted to win almost as much as the rest of us, he had already begun to set his own rules for winning. That rigid dreariness of task and duty didn't seem to muscle his face, and by the third year when most of the survivors had the looks of executives who lift weights on their lunch breaks, Chachie's smile was that of inevitable triumph.

"I came back after my first year with a vengeance. Anybody that even got a compliment by Royal I went after."

(This was after shit drills and Royal's trying to run him off that first spring.)

And, "At first I wasn't aware that I had my scholarship no matter what, and I wasn't ready to give up my chances to get an education at Texas. I was set on survival. My sights weren't set on being an All-American."

Yet Chachie still had a great redshirt year and then as a junior (but only his second year of football eligibility) led the conference in yards per carry (7.0), and gained around 400 total yards. (While playing second team behind a senior all-conference man.)

"I was, of course, greatly encouraged, and Coach Ellington had told me that I had a chance to be a real star. That summer there was a big writeup in my home-town paper tabbing me as a future All-American."

Yet, as Chachie was starring on the field, his thoughts about the proper role of football were crystallizing:

"That third spring Royal and I had discussions to the effect that I could be a big star if I really sacrificed the next two years. He wanted me to sacrifice everything, but I had become more greedy about my education, and I was also determined not to play with injuries.

"My attitude was still the big problem as far as Royal was concerned. Football wasn't everything to me, and I was primarily there to get an education. He was beginning to realize that I wasn't going to fit the mold; he just couldn't have a renegade.

"He wanted me to be a team leader, but I wasn't the rah-rah sort. And I finally realized that if I were going to be any good, I wasn't going to be a team leader, or the strong silent type.

"The spring of my redshirt year I had thrown myself completely into football, went completely into it, all my thoughts were centered around it just like the coaches wanted. I went on scholastic probation and gained fifteen pounds from eating junk out of nervous tension. (Chachie's final average was a 3.1 on a 4.0 system, and nearly all A's after completing his football.) The real me was telling me what a fool I was. I had abdicated responsibility for myself and for the things I held valuable. But there was always something in the back of my head telling me it wouldn't work. It was the best football I'd played and it led to my big sophomore year. But by my third year I had it in perspective. I knew then if they let me play on my terms I'd be good, but I wouldn't play on any other terms."

"What were your terms?"

"My terms were that I'd get an education. That meant doing such things as going to lectures, things which might interfere with studying your playbook at nights and watching films. And if I was injured, I was injured. I wanted to work out from two-thirty to six and that was it, then forget about it the rest of the time. Then when I was injured I didn't want to play anymore until my injury was healed. That didn't mean that I expected to still be number one when I returned, but I still wanted to be given an opportunity when I came back out, not automatically written off for the rest of the year.

"We gave them four years of blood and sweat, and what we were supposed to get back was an education. But if we played ball the way they wanted, the only thing we got back was the possibility of playing pro ball."

"What do you think Royal thought of you?"

"I had and have no idea. He indicated to me that I was a good football player."

"What did you think of Royal?"

"I had no respect for him as a human being. I felt he'd

sacrificed his whole life to be a great football coach. I respected him as a coach and a judge of athletic ability, but
he was totally impersonal. We were so many head of cattle
and he was going to milk us for all he could. It was a business proposition and they ought to admit it. It was a fraud.
In the pros you know it's a business. If you're the kind of
guy who wants to get a good education and play ball, but
not professional ball, you can't.

  "He wanted to be Coach of the Year and hobnob with
the Governor. What a fraud."

In and Around Moore-Hill

Shape without form, shade without colour
Paralyzed force, gesture without motion.

—T. S. Eliot
"The Hollow Men"

The final spring game of my first spring training at Texas was completed. I was very disappointed with my performance, but as I separated my body from a sweaty uniform, the single fact skipping my mind was no football for four months.

The area outside the dressing rooms was filled with parents, friends, and adulators awaiting their returning warriors. As I left the lockers a cut lip and drooping head helped me tell everyone, "Yeah, I have been to the pits of hell and am man enough to survive, yet I am gracious enough to return to your rather ordinary existence." My parents awaited me with a proud smile.

As we drove back to Denton, thoughts of never having to go back streaked into the spring night. My father hoped that I wasn't discouraged and had confidence that I would make it. It was genuine confidence, as he really believed I could make it, and he gave me substantial support. But underlying this confidence was an acceptance of the winner-loser ground rules. What was not left open was the possibility that I might not really like it—might really want to quit. "You'll get 'em next fall." I pushed myself up against the car door and pretended to fall asleep. I wanted to float away, but what now seemed a very old body held me down. I'd never been more depressed.

As my summer days sped away carrying any relaxation with them, I wanted to retreat somewhere and sort out my real feelings and thoughts from all that was spinning me round. But effective indoctrination works full time, and all summer Coach Royal sent us literature, including a training schedule which began in early June. The rest of this literature was directed toward psyching us with constant reminders that we must always be preparing for what lay ahead. Success in October and November meant hard work in June and July. And if we just kept working—not giving up—at some point in the future somewhere, somehow, it would all be worth it. In the middle of the summer Coach Royal sent us this:

Dear Longhorn:

Getting knocked down is no disgrace; staying there is.
Let me give you the history of defeats one of the great men of all times suffered; yet had the courage to keep coming back:

> Lost job 1832
> Defeated for legislature 1832
> Failed in business 1833
> Elected to legislature 1834
> Sweetheart died 1835
> Had nervous breakdown 1836
> Defeated for Speaker 1838
> Defeated for nomination for Congress 1843
> Elected to Congress 1846
> Lost renomination 1848
> Rejected for land officer 1849
> Defeated for Senate 1854
> Defeated for nomination for Vice-President 1856
> Again defeated for Senate 1858
> In 1860 Abraham Lincoln was elected President
>   of The United States.

It might be that you will start on the third team; drop to the sixth, Or you might start on the first team; drop down to fourth. The question you must answer to yourself is,

"What am I going to do after I am knocked down," Do you pout and feel sorry for yourelf, or do you come back in a fighting mood?

All of you who get on the playing field this fall will be knocked down at one time or another. Never has there been a football player who hasn't been knocked down. The great ones scramble back to their feet as fast as humanly possible; the average football players get up a little slower; the losers stay on the ground.

> Sincerely,

> Darrell Royal

I came back for my second year as a redshirt. (Held out of athletic eligibility for a year to allow for another full year later—this allows the player to grow and add a year's experience, gratis.) Except for five of us, all the others left in my class were also redshirted. This is the most difficult year, because it is a year of limbo. We had not made the exalted place, but some of us hadn't been sentenced to hell yet either. And at no time did we need more emotional support from one another. But during this second year it became vividly clear the premium was on going it alone. I had to prove myself, but I had to do it without emotional needs being satisfied by my teammates. I had nowhere to turn for support. The more unshaky our position the more we had to prove our strength. It was a downward spiral. Our community barely extended to mutual bitching: "Yeah, Coach Campbell made me do so-and-so today—that son-of-a-bitch."

Implicit was, "He can't get to me though—I'm too tough." We did manage to group together on the practice fields before workouts began, and we even came up with special names for the scout teams we were on. (Scout teams, composed mostly of redshirts, ran the coming week's opponent's offensive and defensive alignments against the first three teams.) I was on the offensive attack squad. We wore blue jerseys and called ourselves "The Blue Marauders." Yet, more than anything else, these blue shirts were embarrassments, and the unspoken thoughts were to separate ourselves as soon as possible from those who wore them. Repeatedly someone who had been a charter Marauder became aloofly arrogant when reaching stardom. "I was actually always better than those guys," seemed quite easily to fill the void left by any previous scout team camaraderie. So the basic drive was to separate.

For me this came after the sixth game of the year. Coach Royal selected Leslie Derrick, a third-year man, and myself off the scout teams. We were moved into the varsity room, and I became the only redshirt allowed to dress in this room. I was put on the traveling squad, and then heard from Daddy D. He told me I was going to be playing a lot of football the next three years. Not only had I been physically separated from the rest of the Blue Marauders, but in my gut, I had left them for good.

So basically anything we could have found in each other was eliminated by the total concentration on putting distance between us. And this was not the only way "studitis" affected redshirts. Many of those who had made it wanted to make sure we recognized their superiority. The more they could put us down, the farther removed they could feel from our lonely existence. When we ran plays against them, it was made clear that to hit them with too much enthusiasm would arouse their ire. The message was "How dare you hit me like that. Who do you think you are?" And if a particular redshirt didn't bow to this pres-

sure, they would usually band together to "teach a lesson."
The resister would suddenly find himself being clobbered
from all sides with a little extra intensity. Yet if he let up,
he would have to face the coaches' pressure on him to go
all out. "How do you ever expect to play unless you really
hit somebody?"

The coaches reveled in this disharmony and loved to
produce it. This seemed to be one of the few frivolities in
their serious business.

"Bedrick, are you going to let this redshirt push your ass
all over the field?"—said with the smirk of mock anger.
Then turning to the shrinking redshirt, "All right, really
get after Bedrick this time."

Only problem was, Bedrick and the redshirt were meant
to take this completely seriously—and they did. Otherwise
the humor of the situation would be lost. Occasionally one
of us would get so riled up by these conflicting prods, he
would totally abandon efforts at his own safety and would
go after a first-teamer. But the uppity SOB would usually
pay for it. This daily put-down of redshirts was another
needed prop to hold up struggling egos whose worth was
based on other's weakness. A few, like superstar Tommy
Nobis, now of Atlanta, didn't seem to need it. But others
couldn't seem to get enough of it. They would go to any
point to provoke a Marauder just to be able to reprove their
physical superiority.

Superficially this kind of division might be expected to
wreck a team, but that's only if you completely mistake the
nature of team motivation. This "do anything to stay on
top" was easily translated to Saturday afternoons. Screw
up and there would be someone to take your place Monday. And come game time we were together—not out of
some mutual love, but because each of us needed the other

to keep feeding his own individual worth. We were joined by a compulsive need to win and the mutual enemy who threatened this need.

"A winning team has to be a close-knit crew. We try to draw the players closer and closer together with each day of game preparation, in the same way you would wind a top. The closer to kickoff, the tighter we want that feeling of team togetherness.

"Then we draw the knot even closer. There are other people around us at the hotel, but once we get into the dressing room, the outsiders are trimmed off. It is just the squad, and just before the kickoff, the circle boils down to the guys who are going to do the playing. We want those adrenal glands excited and spurting all sorts of magic substances into the bloodstream and producing an adrenal kick that brings out unexpected strength. The tighter our circle is packed, the bigger the explosion." [1]

This mutual building of hostility that is meant to explode and its underlying fear is referred to as team love and togetherness.

This lack of any real community was most evident in our dorm life. School dormitories are notoriously sterile places anyway, but Moore-Hill was chloroformed vanilla. As I've already mentioned, the football personality inhibits interests in anything not winner-oriented and places a strict taboo on most feelings. The limited human contact that results was best reflected in our everyday language: jock slang. It was aggressive, blunt, very narrow, and extremely unimaginative. The favorite words were "shit, shi-yeet," and "fuck." I know that college men in general aren't sweet-

---

[1] *Darrell Royal Talks Football*, pp. 187-188.

mouthed, but the emphasis on these terms was decidedly greater at Moore-Hill. For one thing with very little to talk about there is not too much need for variety but more importantly, I think it was the easiest way to sound simultaneously aggressive and at ease. There seemed to be some kind of assumed connection between crudeness and toughness.

A very typical conversation which I heard and participated in every day went something like this:

Mack: "Come on in man—what the fuck?" (What are you doing?")

Don: "Hey, you piece of shit!" (Said amiably.)

Mack: "What's wrong with your goddamned ankle, pussy?" (Asking about an ankle hurt in that day's workout.)

Don: "Oh, that fucking Bledsoe kicked the shit out of it today—that big mother-fucker."

Mack laughs, then says, "Sit your ass down, let's play some cards."

Don: "Shi-yeet yow, I'm going to beat your ass today."

This may seem a pretty vivid way of carrying on a simple conversation, but similar exchanges occurred an infinite number of times. This was the limit of our basic interaction. The words varied little and the variation in topics went from jokes to "pussy" to sports. Within this structure it was practically impossible for any of our feelings other than aggression, amiability, and enthusiasm to escape. This limited vocabulary, in turn, reinforced our limited world. If anyone talks the way we did long enough, his emotional range is going to be frustrated, if not forgotten. But for the world we believed in, our language did all that was needed. What others mistook for lack of intelligence was really a frozen life style that could only block and tackle.

I often wonder if part of the reason for hardening the muscles and bulking up in football is to rigidify against feeling. Because feelings (except for a limited few) do not fit in with the football rules of what it means to be a man or a winner. Fear is something to be overcome—not felt. Tenderness is to be avoided at all cost. And in general I couldn't talk to my teammates because I and they took a chance on loosening those muscles and relaxing that structure. I guess this was such a threat that most dared not even attempt it. So I quit trying, played cards, and acted tough.

The emotional barricades in Moore-Hill were also carried into our outside relationships. Here too, spontaneity and involvement were prevented by a total faith in the rules of masculinity. Since being a winner depended on a strict obedience to the right rules, any uncertainty about them could not be tolerated. So when these maxims weren't specific, we usually created our own derivatives. For example, my "five-date rule." After breaking off my relationship with my high school girlfriend Gail, I dated a number of girls. But to make certain I avoided any involvement, the maximum number of times I dated a girl was five. At the time I rationalized this by telling myself, "I'm a stud playing the field and anything more than five might interefere." Dating a girl any longer than this meant to possibly lose control of the situation; to lose control was to be weak. To be weak was not to be a man. As a result, I never really knew a girl in my four years of college.

This absence of any real involvement extended into all parts of our social lives. The men's fraternities rushed all jocks, especially football players, but again our masculine myth provided us with an emotional limbo. It was real prestige for these frats to have us as members (so much that a few offered membership for nothing), but I quickly sensed that we were basically to be their celebrity displays. Any personal contact was minimized. On the one hand we football players were bigger than life—stars. On the other hand, we were subhumans, dumb animals. We were for the most part either worshipped or condescended to, yet we were seldom just other people. I felt like the beautiful blonde: guys will do anything to get in her pants, but when she's not around they discuss her lack of brains. And "stupid goddesses" get worshipped or screwed—but not seen or felt. And I had the distinct feeling that we were so wanted by the fraternities because we made it easier for these former high school stars to live out their frustrated glory fantasies.

Such scarcity of emotional contact, despite our footballed muteness, left most of us with plenty of frustrated energy. In fact, at times I had the strange sensation of impending explosion, as if at any moment our tight jacket of profanity would break into crazy gibberish, or en masse we would blindly charge some dummied Moore-Hill wall with all that human beef collapsing those neatly squared bricks. Maybe that's part of the reason why some of my non-athlete friends seemed to have a fear of what football jocks might do, fear that went beyond their physicalness. There seemed to be the idea that you never knew when we might explode, and I don't think this was pure fantasy. Football seemed to keep us at a simmering boil, and what was left over was poorly drained into pranks, roughhousing, and picking on new freshmen.

For me these releases were concentrated into a continual series of practical jokes. Typically, they were aimed at persuading someone of imminent disaster. On one such occasion, the disaster was a case of the "Bavarian ticks." This horrible disease struck a lanky, shy, and nervous freshman basketball player who had quit the team and now lived off campus. His name was Jim Smith.[1] Without warning, Jim, a naïve and perpetual worrier, suffered a sudden Bavarian tick attack at three in the morning. Being the only other person present at the time, I was first to notice it.

"Jim, what are those little bumps on your legs?"—small, red marks left on his upper thighs from a vicious towel fight thirty minutes earlier.

"What bumps?"

"These little things here . . . Jesus, what are those?"

"Oh, shit man, they're just bumps."

"They look just like stuff my old roommate . . . naw, I'm sure they're not that . . ."

"You're sure they're not what?"

"Man, they're probably nothing—don't worry about it . . . they just kind of look like something my old roommate used to have . . . but I'm sure you couldn't have that."

"Couldn't have what?"

"Oh, you have to live practically in filth to even get it, so I wouldn't even worry." (Jim's room was notoriously dirty and he never washed his sheets, which at the present moment were a murky yellow.)

"What, goddam it? Couldn't have what?"

"Oh, I was just talking about my old roomie. He caught a rare tick disease—I think they called it Bavarian ticks—but he was always real dirty. They apparently thrive on that . . . the son-of-a-bitch was in the hospital for two weeks. They said if he'd come in a day later he'd been a goner. I think you have about three days, after one of those fuckers bites you, to get to a doctor . . . I think they get in your blood."

---

[1] a pseudonym

"Well, did your roommate get okay?" Jim was starting to get a very serious look on his face.

"Yow—and boy, you should see how clean he keeps his goddam place now."

"What did they look like?"

I hesitated and then looked at his thighs . . . "To tell you the truth, Jim, they looked just like these bumps—but I'm sure . . . Then I looked at his filthy sheets as if discovering them for the first time. "Goddam! Man, when's the last time you washed your sheets?"

"Long time . . ."

"Do your legs itch?"

"Yow, they kinda do."

"Listen man, this ain't anything to fuck around with— I'm not trying to scare you but I think you got exactly what my roommate had . . . the Bavarian ticks! We'd better get your ass to the doctor right now."

"But it's three-thirty in the morning."

"Listen, you cannot fuck around with this shit—get dressed and I'll drive you."

Now Jim was really nervous and as he was getting dressed I noticed another bump on the back of his neck. A pimple. "Goddam, man, you've got another one on the back of your neck. Jesus Christ! How dirty *is* your bed? Let's go!"

We drove to the student health center which, of course, is closed at three-thirty in the morning and has only a night buzzer for emergencies. We rang the night bell and a nurse hurried down.

"You need to get my friend here to the nurse's station quick."

Jim now looked totally petrified and I could hardly keep

from breaking up. He walked into the nurse's station and I stayed outside in the hall—close enough to hear.

Nurse: "Yes, what is it?"

"Well, ma'am . . . I've got . . . well my friend . . . my friend's roommate had it. Well, ma'am, I think I've got . . . well, I've got the Bavarian ticks!"

"The what?"

"The Bavarian ticks—they're all over my legs."

"Well, ah, ah, Mr. Smith . . . pull down your pants and let's see the problem."

Jim was too shy to pull down his pants and quickly said, "Well, I've got one on the back of my neck too."

The nurse then briefly examined him and very stiffly said, "Mr. Smith, we only handle emergency cases at this time in the morning, but if this problem persists I suggest you see a doctor tomorrow."

I don't know if she figured he was the victim of a joke and was being sympathetic or was just scared, but she said no more. In the meantime I had collapsed from laughter. The next morning the bumps had gone away but his embarrassment hadn't.

By the time I was a sophomore this type of humor was my specialty. These practical jokes just seemed a normal extension of the rest of my life. Their cruel undertone pervaded nearly all of my contact with other players. But even more than being obvious examples of frustration and hostility, these instances were pathetic. They were pathetic because, except for football and occasional sex, my total expression of feelings was practical jokes.

The manipulative use of these unexpressed feelings kept me and most of my teammates ready to explode at the proper snap count. But who is to say what would have happened if we 250-pound puppets had broken the strings and put this imposed explosion to our own ends. Maybe for one thing, these dreary marines called coaches could no longer construct human torpedoes out of lost love.

Tejas Club

There was always such a contrast between what our lives really were and what they seemed to others. To most students we were either dumb jocks or distant heroes. As heroes we represented some American myth about the ideal man. This was especially evident during the football season when we were most in the limelight.

There is something very private about a bonfire whistling into a cool autumn night, but Texas students always seemed driven to fill any privacy with the social balm of big groups. A huge bonfire and pep rally was an annual affair prior to the Texas-Texas A & M game. This rally, like most Texas pep rallies, always brought an enormous crowd. One in 1964 had at least ten thousand people. (At a pep rally prior to the Texas-Arkansas game of 1969, there were thirty to forty thousand including LBJ, the governor, and most of the state's top officials.) These rallies were centered around a specially erected wooden stage where Royal, the team, and other public notables gathered for presentation. Perched atop this wooden Texas temple as the honored warriors, we players and Daddy D had the look of religious solemnity while pitched excitement filled the eyes of all around us.

Directly below us and exuberantly swirling to Texas howls were smiling, unmarked cheerleaders. They danced to the Texas band which was behind them, dressed in gaudy orange uniforms, while the flight of fire ricocheted off the beautiful Colorado River not more than one hundred yards away. Also in our immediate view were about fifty young men who called themselves the "Cowboys." They were considered part of the campus elite and stood to one side in

160

their self-conscious western outfits. They had brought their campus starlets and spurs, windblown neckerchiefs, chaps and clumsy boots from another day, and were the one group who looked as if they knew us well. And indeed they did, since a high percentage of their members had came from the ranks of the players now sitting above them. They were best known for their tough initiations, which included the use of an electric cow prod and the paddle whipping of each new member until blood was drawn from his bare ass. At one time these Cowboys had sizzled their new members with a branding iron, but the school had long ago banned this practice following a branding infection that resulted in death. But now they were a little less frenzied than the rest of the crowd as they seemed to feel that they should have at least one foot on stage.

This big occasion and its excited perfumed yells had been preceded that afternoon by carefully made floats and victory signs, beer busts and barbecues; and now their sorority and fraternity owners were holding hands and intensely drawing one another toward our center stage. "Go Longhorns, go Horns—go!" and these coded words sent aloft by the roar of thousands sparked some strange electricity that went far beyond any social frivolity. "We're Number One! We're Number One!" kept spontaneously breaking out, interfering with the more organized cheers. Then came the biggest ovation with the introduction of Royal, a tremendous awe and respect flowing from this nineteen- and twenty-year-old audience.

"You are a very important part of this team." (Screams and yells.) "We need your support . . . and with it we'll take A & M." (Great yelling.)

Everything Royal said was confident, assured, with the air of "We're ready—it will be tough, but we're ready."

And it was obvious his audience felt honored to be a part—
to be a part of Number One and the best. As he finished,
the band struck up the Texas fight song, and I couldn't help
but feel we players were superior to those around us.

As a redshirt I attended the games just like the other students—with a date and a student ID. Yet even in the stands
I was not an ordinary student.

"How tough is he, Shaw? Have you ever hit him?"

"Awwww, he's all right . . . nothing special." And, of
course, when my date would ask how we all kept from getting hurt, I would only coolly shrug my shoulders.

Thirty minutes before a Texas game the stands were always colorfully jammed, with the stadium field presenting
a rich menu of the biggest and best: "Big Bertha," the
world's largest drum, the Texas band, "biggest showband
in the Southwest," and, of course, the best team in the land.
Nothing short of Number One would do, and after each
victory the fans would again break into "We're Number
One! We're Number One!" Everywhere I could see big
stetsons and orange string ties monogrammed with a neatly
printed "Hook 'em Horns." We all had our "Hook 'em"
signs up—the index and little fingers sticking straight up in
the air with the others held in the palm of the hand. The
idea was to wave these two fingers and yell, "Hook 'em
Horns, hook 'em." On the way to the games the fans would
give each other the sign to identify themselves. And there
was something very humorous about seeing thousands of
overweight middle-aged men with their orange ties putting
abandoned forgotten energy into two protruding fingers.
Yet for reasons not really understood then, the humor I
felt at these scenes was mixed with a vague feeling of sad-
ness.

As the time neared for my teammates to come onto the

field, the cheerleaders and Cowboys converged on their entrance point. These were the times I most wanted to be down there. As the crowd drew sight of the first burnt-orange jersey, it came to its feet in an atmosphere, though tense, almost carnival in its excitement. Yet very soon it would be clear that this parochial energy around me went much deeper than stetson hats and cheerleaders. As the band began the school song, "The Eyes of Texas," a complete, total seriousness would swallow this massive architecture. No church hymnal could arouse as many misty eyes and the warm communal feeling that momentarily existed. And sometimes I even felt that all these frenetic Texas exes came back for one reason: to sing "The Eyes of Texas." It was as if this was a way of reassuring themselves that their American dream was real. Even if they had lost faith in their own ability to conquer and defeat, they could watch us Supermen and feel that their beliefs were at least still possible.

When victory came, everyone looked to the campus tower and waited for its top to turn bright orange. As I drove my date back to her palatial sorority house, in only my second year of being a Longhorn, I had the strangest feeling that something was missing.

As this second year at Texas continued, I began to feel I had to get some other connections—connect to someone or something outside football.

Believing any change in environment would help, I asked Coach Royal for permission to live outside the dorm my third year. To get permission we had to be entering at least our junior year (scholastically) and be on the approved list—right attitudes, good grades, and so on. Even with the right qualifications leaving Moore-Hill was definitely discouraged by the meager fifty-five dollars a month we were

given to cover all our expenses. Royal had said, "We like
to keep them all together. They don't get so distracted."
Still, I met all the right tests, and after agreeing to main-
tain my previous discipline, I was allowed to leave Moore-
Hill.

I decided that I would live in the Tejas Club, a small
campus male organization that was academically oriented
I had eaten there several times and was amazed at the members' dinner manner and dialogue. The mood was friendly
and casual; there was no rushing for chairs or grabbing for
meat. The waiters were members themselves and the cook,
Gwen, was a special charter member—a woman who had
been with the club for twenty-five years. The dining hall
had room for only about thirty chairs and this small size
gave the place a feeling of intimacy. The conversation was
good-natured and wide-ranging, and I thoroughly liked the
idea of being the club's only varsity athlete.

So with my third year approaching, I was peeking through
a few openings in my future. I had just finished a successful
second spring training (starting for one side in the final
Orange-White spring game) and should begin playing for
the varsity, which rather than ecstasy brought relief. But
even more importantly, I would be living outside Moore-
Hill Hall. Maybe my world was going to expand beyond an
oval spiral football.

I went to Austin my third fall in shape—ready to go.

I didn't get past the physical examination. The team doctor discovered I had a heart murmur and thought it needed
closer inspection. After I'd seen several heart specialists, it
was determined that I had a hole in my heart and would
need open-heart surgery. A cardiac catheterization (putting a tube and fluorescent fluid into the heart) was to
be done to verify this diagnosis. This whole process of

seeing heart specialists and having the catheterization took six to eight weeks. Then it was decided, after the catheterization, that I didn't have a hole after all, and would not need an operation. Yet the time spent had knocked me out of at least half the football season. But I learned something from this incident. It finally started sinking in that Royal and the rest of the coaches had no interest in me as a person. After they found out that I would miss at least several weeks of the season and would most likely be through with football, I didn't hear from them again. During those weeks there were no questions, no inquiries into my condition. Once my name had been removed from the chart, I ceased to exist. When I did come back, the extent of their concern seemed to be in how fast I could be back to some productive use. From this point on, I found it increasingly difficult to be totally dedicated.

Along with this growing realization that Daddy D had no concern for me came another discovery. I wasn't ready to give up my football props. Just joining myself to a new environment did not rid me of my driving psyche. I was still carrying its mental baggage around inside of me. Not only did I have my same motivational core, but I also discovered how much I depended on the social knowledge that I was a Texas football player. For me to go somewhere without this knowledge was to go naked. But most of my new acquaintances, for their own reasons, made sure I was protected. A typical introduction—especially to a girl— went something like this: "This is Gary, a Tejas member . . . Gary plays on the football team." And after a brief pause or chuckle, "And he's not the typical dumb jock either." I was something special—a jock with minimal brains. But still what made me special was that I was a jock with brains, not that I had any. I was a jock, and an exception in that I also did other things atypical of jocks. This actually tightened the hold of my football identity. I became that much more dependent on it for being successful. It was as if all my other qualities would collapse if I lost my jockhood.

Yet my dependence on this Moore-Hill mentality was mostly present in more subtle ways. I attempted to interact with other Tejas members, but invariably I kept trying to defeat them. Of course, these efforts were coated with social congeniality, but nonetheless, my unspoken aim was to win. In most discussions and disagreements I used my mind as an intellectual forearm. And underneath these attempts to overpower I felt the same foreboding that drove me in football. I had a vague sense of futile desperation, as if I was only delaying some inevitable loss. This ominous feeling paradoxically led to more efforts at winning—scoring with girls, being the wittiest, making an A—until I often felt near some explosion.

The stimulation of the Tejas Club was certainly greater than Moore-Hill, yet I still found something missing. I felt just as empty as I had in Moore-Hill. I didn't know why, and it never occurred to me the problem was not in the Tejas Club.

Just when I was most perplexed, word came that my heart was okay and I could return to workouts. With great relief I went back to something familiar—football.

In just a week we would be playing Oklahoma, and although I'd only been on the field a few days I was going to get a chance to play in my first varsity game. I was amazed at how quickly my old psyche came back.

The Game

We were number one. Oklahoma would try to take it from us. Coach Royal is grim as he always is before a game. Still ninety minutes before kickoff, but I'm already up.

I pull my orange-and-white jersey down hard and plant it between my legs. My helmet is polished and there are longhorns pasted on its sides. As I fit my head behind its facial bars and stiff elastic, I stare in the mirror. My right hand is wrapped and I have one elbow pad on. My shoulder pads are so big they seem to push out against the locker-room walls. I keep jamming thoughts out of my mind and sit down to wait.

"Alright men."

I stand up on metal cleats and line up at the door.

I start down the ramp and can feel the broken rhythm of a hundred separate feet. The crowd hasn't seen us yet. But within moments there is a rapid ricochet of cleats, slapped asses and cracking voices.

"Let's get those sons of bitches, Horns! Let's go!"

I feel I'm assaulting the sidelines not just heading toward them. I'm already punishing the grass below me, and the noise above me is hard—a rock band trapped and out of control. And when the Texas cannon explodes, the "amps" are turned loose.

"Hit somebody! Hit somebody!"

Those crazy son-of-a-bitch Sooner players are halfway across the field waving their fists and shooting the bird.

T.V. cameras and 75,000 people, concrete and bands, fans and orange, cheerleaders and red panties, referees and loud numbers, furious coaches and chalked grass, public speakers and Royal's mouth . . .

Hit!—as I lined up for the kickoff, I was ready.

Seventy-five thousand people were on their feet and looking down. After the kickoff my first ten steps were consumed by one thought: *Don't screw up!* Past those ten yards my entire focus was on looking for the ball-carrier. "Get that son-of-a-bitch—get him!"

I avoided my blocker and was the first man down the field. When I looked up the ball had rolled out of the end zone. Leaving the field, I was slapping members of the first team and screaming, "Get 'em, Horns! Put it to 'em. Get their ass!" Reaching the sidelines, I was still in a frenzy, and I kept pacing and yelling for another five minutes. Finally, momentarily exhausted, I calmed down, and began to play the role of a reserve lineman.

My reserve lineman role was only one of the many acted out on the sidelines. The most amazing thing about our games was how everything was done according to standard form. We knew how to act when we were ahead and how to act when we were behind. Within this general breakdown there were distinctions between starters and reserves, offense and defense, backs and linemen, coaches and trainers, and all those various roles were very predictable.

There were a few things that Daddy D was always doing during a game—chewing gum, pacing back and forth, licking his fingertips, and repeatedly saying to those of us not on the field, "Now, men, get back off the sidelines."

Otherwise his behavior when we were ahead was noticeably different from his behavior when we were behind. (Tied games were responded to as losses.) When we were ahead, Royal would nearly always get a blade of grass to chew on. During this winning period his look would be one of serious and earnest intent. His pacing wasn't nearly as fast as when we were losing, and he would often come to a standstill while putting his hands on his hips, as if strutting. When we were ahead, his directions to a player were technical, slow, and in a subdued tone.

When we were behind, Daddy D's rituals changed dramatically. For instance, if he wanted some player he would whirl around and yell "Smith! Smith!" When Smith rushed up to Royal's side, Daddy D would yank him close, grabbing him under the top of the shoulder pads. With teeth clenched, he'd growl a play and hurl Smith toward the field. When Smith was called forward he usually wasn't wearing his headgear, and he'd still be trying to get it on halfway across the field.

Also, while invariably increasing his pace, Royal would begin spitting periodically at the turf. Then, looking like a man with a million thoughts running through his head, he'd grab the headphones from the back-up quarterback or an assistant coach.

The players' form was just as predictable. When first-teamers came off the field winning, they sat down on the benches and threw their helmets between their legs. Then while all the also-rans came over and slapped congratulations, the first-teamers would begin giving orders to everyone around them. While ahead, they sat individually, chewed on ice and drank some saline solution (we always called it green shit). Periodically someone would be hollering at the trainer, "Trainer, bring me some of that green shit." The offensive backs would be the only ones who moved a great deal. They were the showboats and would walk from one end of the bench to the other, helmets off and sure to be in full view. They also seemed the ones most conscious of the fans when running off the field. If one of them had made a long run and was being replaced, he'd take his time before heading toward the sidelines. Players in the huddle almost invariably see a substitute coming in, and there is little question about whom he is replacing. But if a back waited until he was officially told in the huddle, he would then be able to enjoy his applause to a solitary exit. And once to the sidelines he could occasionally hear people call down from the stands, "Great run, Joe!" The offensive backs would also be the only ones to walk over to get their own saline. And while they were walking by, we reserves congratulated them more than anyone else. "Great run, Helms!"

"Yow, we're pushing their ass all over the field," Helms would say.

The offensive line was usually the most humble group. They would throw their helmets down, rest their heads in their hands, and look weary.

But when we were behind, everyone looked more tired. We didn't shout as loud, but were more earnest. The defense would then get together and talk in a circle off to the side. The side chosen was always the one nearest to the game action. The offensive line would kneel anxiously on the sidelines, trading pep talk, whereas the quarterback and a couple of the backs would be crowded around Royal.

During the whole game (whether ahead or behind) Medina would be racing back and forth giving his Medina lectures. But it was when we were behind that Frank became most vocal. He would go around slapping asses and talking to each starter individually.

"You can do it, men. You can do it! Now's the time to do it. Show 'em you're champions. Show 'em you're champions. Now's the time, men."

Yet when Frank was giving his individual speeches, he made sure to stay well behind the coaches.

For a reserve, the most important thing to do was to act ever ready.

"Keep your mind on the game at all times. Know the down and situation. You never know when you will be called."

Periodically a reserve's attention might stray from the action on the field to the girls in the stands. But he had to beware that a coach didn't catch him looking away from the game.

Most of the time the reserves tried to keep up a steady chatter of encouragement. The encouragement was usually a combination of fake enthusiasm and wishful thinking.

Our remarks about the game were generally criticisms of various starters' performance. If a guy we didn't like was screwing up, we'd say, "Smith is really fuckin' up. They're running all over his ass." If it was someone we liked, we'd sympathize. "Boy, John's having a rough time out there today—must really be tough."

For most of the reserves the scary thing was to be called in suddenly without warning. It doesn't give you time to get your psyche up.

That happened to me in the fourth quarter—with us ahead 19–0. Yet, once I was out there, there was no fear of hitting or getting hurt. Instead, my only feeling was apprehension about performing well. I was playing defensive tackle. On the second play I helped throw the ball carrier for a three-yard loss, and I was suddenly conscious of the stands. The noise was a loud buzzing sound of approval. I felt on display and I wanted to throw the quarterback for a huge loss. The next play, the defense came out of the game.

Heading for the showers, I felt tougher and meaner than I had before the game—even though I'd played only briefly. As I entered the locker room I remember thinking, I'm going to be a mean son-of-a-bitch by next year. I smiled at the thought.

Once in the dressing room, Royal gave us a brief talk (he always did this before reporters or others came in). We showered, picked up the box lunch in our lockers—fried chicken, Coke, and a big red apple—and then went to meet girlfriends and fans. As we swaggered out we would try to look humble.

I remember thinking, on the way back to Austin, how much simpler it seemed to put everything into football. Trying to get into other activities like the Tejas Club was merely frustrating. Finally, as we reached Austin, I said to myself, "To hell with all that other shit, I'm concentrating on football. I'm going to be a starter by spring training."

Ten days after the Oklahoma game I hurt my leg and was out for the season.

Now I was left in my new surroundings of the Tejas Club without a chance to prove myself in football until spring.

The Big Man

Left without football again, making it with girls became an even bigger goal for me than it had been when I was in Moore-Hill. Part of this increased need for sexual conquest was because I was no longer proving myself on the field. And in addition I felt I needed to perform for my non-jock Tejas friends. They expected me as a football player to be a stud with women. Given football players' hangups about their masculinity, girls and sex, this became my major touchdown in an already pressure-laden area.

Not only did I feel I had to screw the prettiest women on campus, and score higher than anyone else, but I also had to dominate in the football mold. This meant total toughness, aggressiveness, and no toleration for any of my passivity and softness. So I carried my football view of the world into personal relationships, and instead of going to the movies with a woman, I should have taken an NFL football.

This same compulsive need to dominate led most of my teammates to pursue girls who, at least on the surface, seemed safely unaggressive; the type that swooned over their "big man" and did what he wanted with no back talk. Their discussions about these girls were a funny mixture of disregard and fear. Listeners would have thought these creatures to be participants in a stock show who somehow induced mysterious awe. "You can't let a good-looking piece get to you or she'll scramble your mind."

Yet it was this strong-man act that actually made us so vulnerable. Our superiority depended much less on what we were than on what the female wasn't. We were strong because they were weak. And the interesting paradox was that the weaker we made the girl, the more powerful we made her—because we became more and more dependent on her doing exactly what we said.

And, of course, there are millions of American men who respond to females (and to one another) in this same fashion, yet who never played college football. The point is that football not only encourages but epitomizes this extremely neurotic male personality. And on the whole, my football teammates talked about and treated women as prime beef more regularly than other college men.

And so I found myself dating every night and yet finding not a single satisfactory relationship. As soon as we went to bed the challenge was over, and I was bored. I had to set a new goal—another girl and another victory. I couldn't understand why I was never satisfied. I kept thinking that all I needed was another and better victory—up the ante—maybe by dating a prettier girl. Sometimes I even gave myself a psyche job before I went out: Gotta get up for my date, get in the right mood, as if I were getting ready for a big game.

It was after a date, my fourteenth in a fourteen-day period, that I had my worst moment in college. I was leaving one of those Southern white-columned mansions called a sorority house late one Saturday after a winning night. The street was spilling over with drunks, pretty laughing coeds, and shiny new cars. The sky was perfectly clear and on such nights I had a habit of looking for the Little Dipper. As I was looking up and wondering how much I'd impressed my date on this cool autumn night, something horrible seemed to come from way past those tiny white dots. And carried by the speed of light it passed completely through me before I could turn my head. What it left went beyond emptiness and fear . . . into panic, and for one very stretched moment, I knew I was alone.

The rest of the night I kept moving through Austin. I would walk until this feeling began to tie my stomach again; then I would run, run hard until out of breath. I didn't know what was wrong and I didn't care; I just wanted to be rid of that feeling. Finally, at five in the morning, the calmness of exhaustion had led me back to my room and sleep. Somewhere beyond my dreams that night was eliminated . . . and it was almost a year before I was to remember it.

The American male who ceaselessly pushes himself to the top, while trying to score as the office stud on the side, is going in the same direction I was. This same inner belief of "what makes a man" is also what creates millions of fanatical fans in America who, under the right circumstances, would have been on the field with us. We have surrendered our identities to some stereotyped stallion gone mad. And the more this horse seems to be disappearing from our culture, the more fervidly we cling to the saddle. The new institutional representative and spokesman for this horse has become American sports, especially football. So what I was caught up in was the extreme of what most of us American men are caught up in, and I couldn't seem to disentangle myself. Football was not just an activity for me, it had become my way of dealing with life—"playing the game." I played to win at everything, which meant I could never let down my defense for a moment for fear an opponent would score against me; and as a result, like most American men I was basically without real human contact, alone and scared. The more threatened I felt as I began to wander away from my ego pump, football, the more I felt I had to score somewhere else.

Maybe this is the biggest reason why many never leave football, although while in its grips they are never really secure as men. Though they have to constantly prove themselves on the field, at least there they know the rules well, and they're good enough to win frequently. Whereas to leave this world would only mean that they would have to score somewhere else in a more uncertain, less controlled environment. And football will continue to have appeal to those not in it for this same reason. They envy football players because their rules for being a man are clear—in football you know when you've won or lost, unlike many of their work-life encounters. But they fail to see that a clear-cut victory leads only to another challenge in a perpetual rat race, even more restricting than the one they're in. As long as there is an attempt to hold on to this simple view of life as a series of challenges and victories with a few winners and many losers, then we will be trapped in an anxious and basically frustrating existence. This threat and anxiety will increase as the challenges to this kind of identity multiply, making it ever harder to define winning and losing situations. Thus, with an increasing scarcity of possible victories, there will be an increasing desperation for victory and male glory.

Yet more women are telling us that they are not prizes or trophies won through competitive enterprise. It is becoming increasingly difficult to determine winning and losing in occupations. We are beginning to see the folly in winning the world for democracy by defeating foreign foes, and a "new culture" that stresses community and cooperation continues to grow. What are we to do? Maybe all of us foolish enough to try to hold on to our winning masculine myth will become fanatical football players. The entire adult male population can then bash each other in anguished frustration, and in final desperation we'll devise "National

Shit Drills"—determining from the outset that only one percent are to survive these drills, and at their conclusion this one per cent will be defined winners and real men. Of course, this elite will need to remain ever fit as innumerable offspring and new challengers will be eager to test them. Then finally, when each of us has eliminated the other, the losing survivors can retire to the sidelines in shame and completely surrender the new world to women.

In the meantime while we're all trying to win our personal Super Bowls and struggling to keep our glory fantasies breathing, the less flexible we'll be to these changes and we'll find ourselves in the same kind of bind I was in.

Sadly, most football players seem just as driven all their life; there are never enough victories. This past year the Dallas Cowboys went to the top of professional football, yet the Super Bowl was barely over when their talk turned to the next year and desires of a dynasty. After football they must win at getting the most money, selling the most insurance—drive, drive, and in the background some high school alma mater plays on. Like cotton candy there is never enough until finally, if you're lucky, your system throws up from a total lack of nutrition. But this cotton rot is the eternal prize held in front of the donkey. And supporting this donkey's powerful reluctance to quit his running is the inability to admit that his achieved tastes of victory were not worth the price—not worth the unpleasant experiences that were required to get there.[1] "Everybody wants to win —some just can't pay the price." What if we all simply decide it ain't worth it?

Some of these new thoughts were starting to push in on me. But at the same time interest in Royal and the team

---

[1] Slater, *Pursuit of Loneliness.*

was such that I found it easy to draw a crowd, especially women, into my new surroundings. At first I enjoyed it, yet increasingly this left me empty. So I began going back and forth from encouraging to discouraging this kind of interaction in a shaky alliance.

I was approaching my third spring and another spring training. As the spring semester began, this tug of war accelerated. Occasionally, I would get a full clear flash of how badly I hated it. *I want out* would jar my brain and light my whole body. The intensity of these feelings terrified me, and immediate flashbacks would pop them out. "These new thoughts are really screwing me up. Get them out of your head or you won't be worth a damn for spring training." For the first time I began to have drunken binges. I felt I was losing control. Like so many in similar situations, I overreacted in the opposite direction. I volunteered as a third-year man for Medina sessions. I was putting myself under the most extreme external controls because the inner ones were falling apart. I had missed most of the third fall so my status would be as fourth-year man (junior-athletic-wise) who had played little varsity ball. To fall that much behind with all the fresh meat coming up usually meant dismissal. The first day of spring training I was listed sixth-team left guard. And by this third spring most of my old teammates were gone (less than twenty were left). "Get out of it, get out of it" was pulling ever heavier.

But all the old pressures were still yanking me the other way. And, along with these, a new one had been added. Most of my new friends in the Tejas Club were watching my performance. "Are you going to be starting next year, Shaw? What team were you on today?" It was unbearable for me to say sixth team. So I sucked it up one more time . . . and started working back up. By the last week I had reached second team and was challenging sophomore Danny Abbott for first team. Before our final spring game, Coach Zapalac said that he really liked my effort, and that I now had a chance to beat out Abbott. "He has a little more natural ability [Abbott was later to be named all S.W.C. guard two years running] so you'll have to try harder." More work—more . . . more . . . more.

By this third spring there were fifteen of the original forty-four of us left. And during this spring I was to see Rusty finally check it in. He was a walking medical center, was uselessly beat in shit drills, and Campbell had called him gutless, his voice echoing across a late afternoon. When Rusty quit, I slipped farther away . . . and worked more frantically. Through the melancholy of his departure I did manage to give myself a small pride injection with the thought that I'd outlasted him.

The rest of that spring training was a daze except for one instance that was to linger after all else died. Chachie and Daddy D were the central figures.

Chachie had seen considerable action in the fall as a sophomore, athletic-wise, and was considered the likely fullback starter our next season. However, through his third year, our conversations together had increased in frequency and intensity. He had repeatedly told me that he no longer would belong to the coaches as simply another head of cattle. He was a student before a football player, and a person before a student. He would give full effort when on the field, but otherwise he didn't belong to them. He also said that he would not go through shit drills again, and if hurt he would not play until well. And that henceforth he would have no hesitation about making these points clear to Daddy D.

I agreed, but deep down thought it was no more than words. But for Chachie this third spring, these words were translated into defiance. He had been running first-team full-back when he was injured in a Thursday workout before a Saturday scrimmage. He had been kicked just below the knee on the shin. The top skin barely had a hole, but under-neath the skin had split, and the muscle had stretched and bulged.

"It was a terrible bruise—the slightest touch was really painful. I was number-one fullback at that time. I told them that I couldn't play and the trainers said that they agreed that it was serious and I should stay off it." But an important Saturday scrimmage was coming up.

"We're so short in personnel," Coach Ellington said, "just go in there and do what you can; you won't have to carry the ball—just run the best you can. We need someone to stand in."

"I tried to carry the ball a couple of times anyway, but it hurt so bad I didn't anymore."

When Royal saw the films, he went into a rage. Chachie explained to him during the films what Ellington had told him, and that if he'd been in there to really play, he wouldn't have gone half speed. But Royal dismissed this—you don't go half speed for any reason. And besides, Royal had be-come increasingly suspicious of Chachie's attitude. When we went out to work out Chachie was placed on a special team by himself (below everyone else) and was given a green jersey that only he wore. With all of us gathered around, Royal proceeded to unleash on him.

"That was the sorriest excuse for football I've ever seen."

"I had a hurt leg."

"That's not where you're hurt, you're hurt right here

[Royal pointed at his own gut]. You're gutless. And unless there's some radical change, you'll never play football for Texas again."

Chachie sat kneeling, never blinked an eye, and amazingly managed to look bored. Royal, now even more enraged, sent him off with Coach Akers, the backfield coach, by himself. All this was obviously intended for total humiliation. The other message was total obedience: "You play when we tell you to and go all out, injured or not." For the rest of us it was a dramatic way of showing us the consequences of straying out of line.

Still, only thirty minutes later, Royal called Chachie from his orange tower. He wanted Chachie to run some plays with the second team, obviously figuring he had learned his lesson. Chachie was a good hundred yards from the rest of us when Royal beckoned. All of us turned expecting a desperate running response and frothed mouth. But Chachie had always been a loner—and there was total silence as he ambled, his stocky body barely trotting. Every twenty yards or so he stopped, walked a couple of yards, and then began his slow trot again. Those hundred yards seemed to be suspended. Chachie's face and movements fit an old man retrieving a stray baseball on a casual Sunday afternoon. My heart was running panicked circles for him. I knew something disastrous was going to happen but I didn't know what. When Chachie finally sauntered within fifteen yards of us, Royal simply threw his hat down in disgust. Chachie continued to stare straight ahead, his pace totally unaffected. The tension on the practice field those two minutes—with the only noise being made by two soft pudgy feet—surpassed any other I've known.

Then it was all over and nothing had happened. Chachie

hadn't been struck dead, swept away, or wiped out. To remove all the weight Daddy D had threatened us with required a simple act. Chachie, of course, was never to really play again, but he still remained standing.

Daddy D

A coach likes to have a lot of those old trained pigs who'll grin and jump right in the slop for him.

—Darrell Royal

I was in Coach Royal's office only twice in my whole college career. The first was in the spring of my freshman year for about a minute. I saw something in his office that symbolized what we were to him. He had a big tack board behind him with little one-inch paper circles pinned on it. It was arranged according to football position from left end to right end. Under each of these positions were these little papers with our names written on them. I remember I was the third circle down under a red block saying *guard*. I can honestly say that I don't think I was ever any more important to Coach Royal than that paper circle tacked up on that board.

To understand big-time college football like that played at Texas, the first thing you have to realize is that it is strictly a business, a business that depends on one goal—winning football games. One of the first and most important factors in a successful business is a good public relations man. First and foremost, that is Coach Royal. This public relations ability requires characteristics that we usually think of as belonging to an adroit politician.

Jimmy Banks, a well-known Texas editor, recently described Coach Royal in an article for *The Texas Star:* "Any candidate for governor who is intelligent enough to merit consideration surely must be deeply grateful for the fact that Darrell Royal, the University of Texas football coach, is not in the race. And the idea that he could have been is not as farfetched as you might think. After all, he is an excellent organizer with a pleasing, persuasive personality; he is blessed with integrity, intelligence, charisma, leadership ability and public speaking skills.

"If you could write the formula for a successful gubernatorial candidate, what would you add? Well, if your name happened to be Darrell Royal, you would insist upon one more ingredient: experience in government. He does not have that—and doesn't seem to want it, although some of his more influential friends have suggested, several times, that he would be an ideal political candidate.

"Experience in politics? He has plenty of that—because nowhere, not even in the governor's race, is there more politics than in serving as head football coach and athletic director of a school such as the University of Texas. You can call it politics or public relations, whichever you prefer; undoubtedly, Royal would prefer to think of it as public relations.

"Whatever you call it, it was recognized last month when Royal became the first sports figure ever to be honored as "Mr. South Texas" at Laredo's famous George Washington's Birthday Celebration.

"After becoming one of the most successful football coaches in the nation, Royal retains the "common touch" resulting from his poverty-plagued "Dust Bowl" days in Oklahoma. He won All-America honors as a quarterback at the University of Oklahoma and he remains the epitome of what most people expect All-America football players to be —even to the point of dressing impeccably, keeping his hair neatly trimmed and his shoes shining like a silver dollar, while not insisting that his players follow his example to the letter.

"Almost a decade ago, while he was serving as governor of Texas, Secretary of the Treasury John Connally said of Royal: 'I would hate to have him for an opponent in a political race because he attends to every little detail, he doesn't make many mistakes and he wins nearly every time he comes to bat.'

"This year's gubernatorial candidates should add a lusty 'Amen! to that. They should be most grateful that those who have tried to talk Royal into running for governor—and these include some of the most influential people in the state—have failed." [1]

In fact, I frequently associate Royal's polished homey smoothness with John Connally—especially because of two similar instances. Connally gave the squad a party in 1964, and as we entered the governor's mansion, each of us introduced ourselves to him. Upon leaving three hours later, he again shook hands with us and called every last one of us (sixty to seventy players in all) by our first names. I was flabbergasted.

Coach Royal met my parents once when I was being recruited as a freshman. Four years later he ran into them after a football game and immediately called them by their first names. Three years after I was gone and a full seven years after first meeting them, Royal saw them at the Denton Country Club. Again, without hesitation, he addressed them by their first names. Maybe, you say, he just has a memory for names and faces. Yet two years after I'd played for him for four years I ran into him on campus and he couldn't recall mine. A player that has come and gone and has no P.R. value is a different case.

(The similarity between Royal and Connally goes beyond these experiences. They run in similar social circles, and together with Lyndon Baines Johnson, are easily the most

[1] Jimmy Banks, "Darrell Royal Would Have Been a Tough Man to Beat for Governor," *The Texas Star,* Vol. I, No. 45, March 19, 1972, p. 2.

popular men in the state—with Royal probably number one. They are both Madison Avenue—Texas style. Both are good-looking, intelligent, smooth—and never personally revealing.)

This public relations ability was used to the hilt, especially when recruiting. Like most politicians, Royal seemed to have the uncanny ability to turn his charm on and off at will. I'll never forget the difference in how Royal and the coaches acted toward me before I signed and after I arrived at Texas. Once we were in hand, the charm suddenly stopped. When we were being recruited there were plenty of smiles and conversation, but once there, it was a "you're going to have to show me" atmosphere. I knew many freshmen who were surprised and bitter at this discrepancy. They naïvely thought that Coach Royal, or the assistant coach who recruited them, had some kind of personal interest in them. Upon arriving at Texas they felt deceived and abandoned.

This personal charm was the same charm that Royal so easily displays on television. I was never able to get over how he could be so indifferent to individuals on the field and then talk about "his boys" on the Darrell Royal Show. That warmth and folksy humor that he took to his TV show was locked in the studio before he came to workouts. Oh, at times he even turned on the charm with the team, but it was with the team as a group, and it usually had a definite purpose—team morale for victory. Not that his charm wasn't pleasing, because it was; it's just that he mostly saved it for people other than his football players.

Royal's P.R. ability was undoubtedly one of the main reasons for his success, and certainly the principal one for his pleasant, warm image. Around friends and family he may genuinely be this way—of this I can't know—but I do know this was not his mode of behavior with us. Because of this contradiction, many of us thought of him as two-faced.

Yet he wasn't about to blow his public image, to ever lose his cool, to forget where he was and what his objectives were. Anything that might hurt this public image wasn't going to be said—he was too much the smooth politician. Roy Edwards, sports writer for the Dallas *Morning News* and a big Royal booster, said it well in one of his articles:

"Now those of us who have spent considerable time around Darrell Royal know that there is no more frustrating undertaking than trying to get Darrell to say something he has no intention of saying. The harder you press and the more contentious you become, the cooler, the calmer, the more imperturbable Royal becomes. I would like to see a Percy Foreman, for example, working on Royal as an adverse witness in one of the famed Houston attorney's big criminal cases. I would have to take Royal." [2]

Edwards meant this as a compliment to Royal's coolness, his ability to keep from getting ruffled and to not say anything that would discredit his image. To me it's just part of the public relations package Royal had assembled to aid in his one goal—winning, and had very little to do with how he treated me or the other players.

The only contact I ever had with any of the coaches was either football-related or disciplinary. Even in the dining room the coaches all sat at one table which was at the head of the room. In fact, my total amount of private interaction with Coach Royal during my four years at Texas would not total three minutes. This was the rule not the exception. Even his saying hello to me was dependent on my field performance. When I was doing well, such as starting as a

---

[2] Dallas *Morning News,* Oct. 22, 1971.

freshman or parts of the next two years, he would say, "Hello, Gary." If I was injured or below the third team he generally only nodded in my direction, if that. Some of the players used to think that there was a "coaching conspiracy," because if they were doing badly Daddy D (and most of the other coaches) seemed to pretend not to see them when they walked by. In retrospect, I don't know if it was so much anger or punishment for poor performance as the fact that we didn't have existence or meaning for them if we performed badly. Our function ceased, and as a result *we* ceased.

The effects of this kind of interaction were striking. After a while I also started varying my greetings to Coach Royal accordingly. If I was doing well I would say, "Hello, Coach" in a firm, full voice. If I was doing poorly I'd kind of duck my head apologetically and half-ashamedly, as if I had no real right to address him. And I would give a very muted and mumbled " 'Um, Coach."

In fact, there seemed only one coach who didn't vary his greetings according to performance. This was the head freshman coach, Bob Schultz. Schultz (now in private business) was the lone leftover from pre-Royal days. In fact, he didn't even look like the other coaches. He had tousled hair, skinny, bony legs, and was always puffing on a pipe. He looked more like the absentminded professor than an efficient, well-drilled "leader." This absentminded look was not a mirage, as Coach Schultz frequently forgot our names. However, he wasn't partial—he forgot starters' names as easily as he forgot those on the sixth team. Yet despite these lapses of memory, he was the only Texas coach who ever asked me how I was doing.

"Larry," he would say—he called me Larry—"Larry, how have things been?"

"Fine, Coach."

"Now Larry, you stick with them and play like you can and you'll be a starter around here."

This absentmindedness also made Schultz the only coach to seem occasionally vulnerable and human. One such instance stands out in my mind. It came at the end of one of our freshman workouts and the day before a big game. All the other coaches had gone into the field house while Schultz remained to give us the pre-game pep talk. As he spoke, we all stood around him in a tight circle. At first, it was a typical "go get 'em" speech. Then a few of us began to smell smoke. Coach Schultz noticed it too because he hesitated briefly and sniffed, as if to say, "What's the smell?" Then as little clouds drifted by our face masks, we couldn't help but look for their source. We soon discovered that these discolored vapors came from a pipe, and this pipe was located in a fast-burning pair of trousers—Coach Schultz's pants were smoldering! But how do you tell your coach in a respectful, subservient manner that he's been ignited? We looked around at each other, and the smoke got thicker until finally one daring freshman, Jim Helms, mumbled, "Coach . . . a . . . a . . . Coach, you're on fire!" Coach Schultz threw his hands to heaven in a St. Vitas dance, while his girlish scream chased evaporating flames into the sky.

"Goddamn! Goddamn!" were his only utterances as he pounded his pants and danced in abandon. Then when our laughter had finally died of exhaustion, Coach Schultz very quietly and very seriously called us closer in. "Men," he said shyly, "do me a favor and don't tell the other coaches—will you?"

That's the closest I ever felt to a coach at Texas.

However, it would not be long before Coach Schultz was

gone. His kind of inefficiency did not fit in with this serious Texas business.

It's one thing to be a grown man getting a job with an organization with no pretense of interest in anything but your performance, but it is a completely different thing to be seventeen or eighteen years old and have a celebrity like Royal come visit you. In the first place, you're awed by his mere presence. And he doesn't say, "I have a money contract here. You will be paid this amount as long as you perform up to certain standards." Instead, he speaks as if he really cares if you get an education, says there's even a brain coach to help you out. And most importantly, once you sign that piece of paper there's no way he or anyone else can take it away from you. And if you can't make it in football, at least you get a free education.

"Yes, Mrs. Shaw, we'll make sure and take good care of your boy."

But he forgets to tell dear Mom and Dad that he can only have one hundred on full scholarship. If running the stands isn't convincing, shit drills should be; and if that doesn't work he is going to call that same son into his office and talk to him a little differently from the way he did in Mom and Dad's living room. In fact, this son will soon wonder how he could have ever even considered keeping his scholarship and eating in the athletic dining room while he's not performing well on the field. A reminder of what others would do for a chance at his scholarship with a subtle inquiry about his manhood should finish the job. That boy who signed his first paper in Mom and Dad's living room is going to sign again, and he's going to be plenty ashamed that he didn't sign sooner. And he's going to duck his head when he leaves that office—the one with the picture of the big

Longhorn behind Royal's chair. And the vibrations from Daddy D are going to tell him that Darrell knows that not everyone can be a winner.

When the son talks to Mom and Dad that night he's going to tell them he's quit football. The reason he'll give is that he's tired of football or that he doesn't have enough time to study. Then he'll tell them that he's decided to give up his scholarship and get a job—it's only right. The in-between events are going to be left out because it's hard enough to tell them that he's a quitter.

Despite its impersonal nature, the relationship between the players and Royal was tied in a multitude of powerful knots. For us, Daddy D was in part the authoritarian father of whom our fear, awe, and respect were ever-present. For example, in the dorm we all had a game where we'd pretend we didn't give a damn what Daddy D thought, said, or did. We'd talk about what a two-faced son-of-a-bitch he was, and in general bad-mouth him. We always tried to give the impression that his opinion didn't matter. But our real feelings —despite earnest efforts at pretense—became obvious when he wanted to talk to one of us (which usually meant goodbye). In those instances he had one of the trainers drop a note in the player's mailbox informing him that he wanted to see him immediately. And if there were several of us in a room together with someone who had gotten a note, we all tried to be blasé. The guy whom the message was for would act tough and pretend he was unafraid.

But unlike an authoritarian father, we were not Royal's children. He would not even punish us as his own, but simply remove us from his playing field. So to us he was the authoritarian of whom we feared disapproval and judgment, but to him we were left guards and right guards, winners and

losers to be used in the eternal quest for victory. In his universe were Arkansas and Oklahoma and men like Frank
Broyles of Arkansas with whom he could play his game of
testing his own virility and power. To be king and capture
national championships you need pawns, and he got them.
For a king to play with pawns' lives, he must be able to
convince them that he has some power—that he can give
them something that they can't give themselves.

The best symbol of his role as judge and overseer was
the orange tower from which he observed most of his workouts. The tower was always in the middle of the practice
field and stretched fifty to sixty feet into the air where Royal
would be perched at the top. When he went up there his
sole companion was a megaphone which he used to dis-
seminate his orders. From this point he could see the whole
field and could yell something at one of the halfbacks, then
a second later could yell at one of the guards clear across
on the other side of the field. To hear this voice coming from
above through a megaphone with the words, "Shaw, get off
on the count," would curl my spine. I would be scared and at
the same time would want to turn around and scream up at
that tower, "Get screwed!" but in my gut that was the
same as shooting God the bird. Also, I could see the effect
on my teammates when he would holler down a simple,
"Good job, Bill." There would be a sudden increased exer-
tion of energy, and if the player was borderline, a panicked
glee would come to his eyes as if to say, "I might make it."

Also, once Daddy D decided to get rid of someone, he
would usually find a way—even if it took a little imagination.
One of the many varied methods was told me by Lowell
Clayton, now an attorney in Austin. At the time, Lowell
was a Moore-Hill dorm counselor, and the particular guy

Royal was having a little trouble getting rid of was Bill
Paschal from San Angelo. (Bill had seriously injured his
neck and his future football potential was in doubt.)

"In the spring of my junior year I was employed by the
University of Texas Housing and Food Services as a resident
counselor for a section of Moore-Hill Hall. Our pay was not
only our room free, but there was an implied honor in living
around some of U.T.'s finest brawn. Our duties were rather
perfunctory, but we were required to keep the noise down,
see to it that no more than a minimum of property was
destroyed, and if there was any real trouble call our head
counselor Larry Phillips or the man above him, Jim Brantigam. Brantigam was the actual man hired to handle all
the real sticky discipline problems and was fairly effective
in doing it. Everyone knew, however, that the real authority
when it came to athletes, regardless of whether they played
football or tennis, was Darrell Royal. It was apparent that
Royal had a great deal to say about all phases of dormitory
life. He not only had all the first-string varsity assigned to
ground-floor rooms, but also allowed them to get away with
more, discipline-wise, than the lesser beings. But Royal's
influence was felt most directly when he would make a
'necessary' visit to the dorm.

"On one such occasion he came to the dorm and chatted
with a few of the counselors. In those days, for a counselor
to have an audience with the coach was quite an honor. I
remember very distinctly his easy bearing and how com-
fortably deliberate he was. He chatted for a while and then
impressed upon us how very appreciative he was that we
were making sure the boys were studying and keeping training (no alcohol in the dorms). He then mentioned just in
passing how much trouble he had with some of the players

and how gentlemanly some of the others were. By way of reference he alluded to Bill Paschal—and how much trouble he could sometimes be. He drifted on to other topics of conversation and eventually weaved his way back to Paschal asking solicitously if we knew of any specific acts of misconduct. He then invited us to come see him if we had any problems, and said that if our parents were in town we should have them drop by to see him—and if we would, look out for anything Paschal might do, and to let him know immediately.

"Now it was rather uncommon for any night to go by without some sort of ruckus. For instance, it was thought to be really cool to wreck the vending machines, or better still see who could carry one of them to his room. Water fights, bottle rolling [rolling Coke bottles down the hall], harassment of black dorm residents, and loud stereos were nightly events.

"But on the particular night in question, someone threw a firecracker into the courtyard of the dorm. The culprit turned out to be Paschal, and Royal was immediately called."

From there Paschal was sent to Dean Franks: "Dean Franks told me that I could be indefinitely suspended," said Paschal, "and I thought he was going to send me before this committee." Paschal luckily managed to avoid disciplinary probation for this offense (for disciplinary probation he could be taken off scholarship) but he was in a position where one more infraction would certainly do him in. And naturally this would have been easy enough to arrange, but all were saved the trouble when Paschal left school his next semester.

Only much later did Bill discover that Royal had gone to all this extra "trouble" for him.

"He never said anything to me—I'm surprised he even thought enough of me to want me gone. I didn't think he knew I existed."

Most of the time these things weren't dealt with even that directly. Most of the ways could be better covered on the surface, made to look as if the actions had no such intent at all. A good example is the way medical attention was handled. On the surface it was impartial, but in practice, as I have stated previously, it was very selective. Members of the first two teams saw a doctor on request and those below had a hell of a time ever seeing one. A prime example of this is what happened to Chachie in his second fall as a red-shirt. He had gotten a tremendous bruise on his calf that was so sore he had difficulty walking. Five straight days he asked Medina if he could see a doctor about it, and Medina, refused saying, "No, it's just a bruise."

"I had gotten kicked on the inside of my calf. This 'bruise' had swollen to the size of a hard ball and was black and blue from my toe to knee. The sixth night after being kicked, my leg was so painful that I couldn't even go to sleep. Then, the next day in the middle of one of my classes, it was hurting so bad I had to get up and leave. Right then I decided, 'Screw Royal,' I was going to see a doctor.

"When I showed the doctor this bruise his immediate reaction was, 'Son-of-a-buck, don't move.' He was afraid that I would loosen the blood clots in my leg—I had a rather serious case of phlebitis. He wouldn't even let me move, and put me in a wheelchair. Then he immediately proceeded to cut on my leg, pulling out the blood clots.

"This injury originally happened on a Monday and it

wasn't until the following Monday that I went to the doctor. He later told me that if I had waited another eighteen hours, I would have probably been dead.

"After this the coaches were real cheery toward me for a while. They never said anything about the injury but just acted like they were glad to see me back."

Suddenly, Chachie's injury had become just one of those "unfortunate instances."

Usually, however, the results of the coaches' treatment were not this dramatic. It was more often just another subtle way of making the "selected ones" feel that it wasn't worth it. More typical was an injury that was not serious but was painful. And with this pain the "selected" could look forward to shit drills that afternoon, all the time knowing Daddy D wanted them gone.

As for physical intimidation, Royal would never place himself in that position; but he wasn't above allowing his assistants this prerogative. For example, Jim Pittman, the late head coach at T.C.U., and at that time offensive line coach at Texas, was known for having literally kicked rear ends when dissatisfied.

Charles Holman, a fellow freshman guard, and I were plenty motivated by Pittman early in our first spring. We were running offensive plays and Holman missed the snap count. While Holman was still bent over, Pittman kicked him in the tail and then threw him down on the ground, screetching at him as he tumbled to the turf.

"Holman, you listen to the goddamn snap count and you'd better not miss another one."

Then he jerked him up off the ground by his face mask and threw him back down again in the direction of the offensive lines.

"Now get up there and do it right."

Holman looked petrified and all he could get out was, "Yes, sir."

This variety of controls gave us the feeling that Royal had supernatural powers over us that we couldn't escape, and yet in our minds to quit as a way of escaping branded us forever. A double bind with no way out.

Another indication of how we weren't really human to Royal was his response to injuries on the field. In high school when someone would get hurt on the field the coaches might try to give the impression of not being concerned to create tough images. They wanted us to think tough and come to realize that injuries were part of the game that had to be overcome. But they obviously noticed and would at least check with the trainers if the injury appeared at all serious—*no matter who* was injured. But more than once I saw Royal totally ignore (seemingly out of complete disinterest) players who seemed to have gotten serious injuries (such as a torn-up knee) right in his field of view. I'm sure seeing innumerable football injuries over the years dulls you somewhat to this, and I wouldn't expect Royal to turn pale. But a total "could care less" attitude seems to be stretching it.

An example of Royal's response to player injuries was told to me by former Texas star George Sauer. Sauer tore the cartilage in his knee in his third year at Texas. It occurred during a spring training scrimmage.

"I remember the day well. Royal had had a meeting and was still in his street clothes when he came onto the field. He must have missed lunch because he had a hamburger in one hand and a Coke in the other. It was almost immediately after his arrival—we were already midway into a scrimmage—that I was injured. I was playing defensive end and Marvin Kristynik [quarterback] was sprinting out around my side. I was just preparing to make the tackle when Joe Dixon [the wingback] cracked back on me. Immediately I went down. It was the most excruciating pain I've ever known. For a while I was just writhing on the ground, totally unconscious of anything around me. When I opened my eyes, the first thing I saw was Royal standing over me with a completely expressionless look, biting into his hamburger. Then I again faded into the pain and continued to pull up grass and roll around until a couple of trainers came to my aid. While they were helping me to my feet and carrying me to the locker room, Royal never said a word to me, never changed expression, and kept eating that damn hamburger. His standing over me with that completely detached look is the most vivid memory I have of him."

Of course, it must be remembered that this was spring training. Injuries in the spring are of less concern because players can recover in time for use in the fall. At least Sauer's injury was recognized by Royal in the fact that he walked over to him. If he had been a player not likely to see action come "turnstile time," Daddy D would not have given him even a second glance.

Perhaps surprisingly, this detachment of Royal's increased his power. He was more unknown, more untouchable, yet still had the final word. The other coaches did nearly all of the individual coaching so we could at least see them sweat a little, but Royal saved his role and words for selective moments which increased their significance. One of these times for me was late in the fall of my second year. I was a redshirt, but had been giving good effort and doing well. Yet I remember being so frustrated because I thought Royal never saw my performance. Then one day before workout, he came up to me and said, "Gary, you're showing a lot of promise, and I expect you to be playing a lot of ball for us the next three years." That's all he said, but I was elated and dazed.

The next day I was moved into the varsity dressing room —the only redshirt given this privilege. Thus, the Act followed the Word. The following day he was back into his completely detached role, and that was the last personal comment I was to hear from him for over a year.

This removed, deified air also made his pep talks more effective. Generally, before a game or at half time he wasn't too much on the rah-rah side. He was more, "We have a serious job to do, and they're going to be tough." So when he chose to do something to fire us up it had exceptional effect. The time I remember best was half time of the Texas A & M game in 1965. We had won the National Championship in 1963, beat Alabama in the Orange Bowl in 1965 and had been 4–0 and ranked number one in the country earlier in the year. Then Arkansas had beaten us 27–24 on a last-minute drive and it seemed to completely demoralize the team. We lost three of our next four and were behind 17–0 at half time against Texas A & M. When we came into the dressing room we were obviously defeated and totally dejected.

Royal, in a proud, dignified manner, told everyone to raise their heads. He said, "Men, it was easy to get out there and play like gladiators when we were fighting for a National Championship—we were in the limelight. But now all we have to fight for is our pride. It would be easy to finish the season by playing out our last thirty minutes with-

out too much effort, especially for you seniors, because
there's really not that much difference between 5-5 and 6-4
records. But now when it's tough and there's nothing but
pride to fight for, you can show your real stuff and that
you're a Longhorn. Men, to win, we're going to have to
keep them from making a single first down—none. And
we're going to have to score three times."

He then turned to the board and wrote 21-17, and
pointed toward it. He then asked all the seniors to get in
line at the door, and told the rest of us to look them straight
in the eye and shake their hands as we left the room. We
were to dedicate the last thirty minutes to them.

I had to fight back the tears and would have jumped off
the upper deck if he'd asked me to. In all our minds there
was no way A & M would make a single first down—and
they didn't. Despite a couple of fumbles, we scored three
times and when it was over the scoreboard read 21-17.
When we got back to the dressing room Royal called us
together and, without saying anything, simply pointed to
the blackboard which still had 21-17 written across it.

Royal and the other coaches seemed to have a sixth sense
of how far to push us; if revolt came too close to the surface
they left the scene. Their message was clear—for us to fight
back meant we might as well quit, and they weren't even
going to be around to notice our departure. In my own experience there were only a few instances when I came close
to revolt, but how the coaches reacted to them stands clearly
in my mind. One such instance occurred in the early part
of my third spring training when I was a lowly sixth-team
guard. The starting offensive line was running plays against
a line of defensive dummies and a live defensive backfield.
The coaches had been riding me, and I was already hostile

when Royal called me over from a guard drill to the defensive backfield.

He said, "Play safety and come up with the flow."

This was mainly practice for the offensive linemen, as
they were to be practicing on their downfield blocks with
myself and a couple of others the targets. Since I'd never
played in the defensive backfield, it was well understood
that in this situation I was a guinea pig.

After the first play Royal yelled at me, "What the hell
are you doing? Come up with the play faster and more to
the side."

At first, I managed to control the immediate anger I felt
by mumbling to myself, "Go to hell." But when the next
play started I headed full blast straight for the offensive
tackle who was to block me. Our solid contact just added
more juice until I could hardly wait to hit him again. I
got ready by setting my feet and drawing back my forearm . . . then I exploded into his midsection. By the time
he had flipped and landed I was losing control. Now I
couldn't even wait for him. The next play I met him five
yards off the line cussing and swing both elbows. Then something in me completely broke. Before the next play had
even started I was charging full speed into the line of scrimmage screaming and crying in a frenzied rage . . . and
just at this point, Daddy D responded in a completely calm
monotone, "Shaw, you can go back to your other drill
now."

As soon as he'd said this he turned to the quarterback
to show him what he'd done wrong on the last play.

I turned and walked to the other drill—totally limp.

The next day when I came to workout I looked up at
the position charts and I'd moved up three teams and was

now on the third team. Royal had gotten what he wanted and had known exactly when to cut it off. Instead of a revolt, he had used my anger to his own ends of making me a "better player."

This ability to motivate is an example of why Daddy D has been so successful. But, of course, there are several parts to Royal's success—even though all have the common origin of his complete dedication to winning. Another obvious part is his rather substantial organizational capacity (including picking assistants just as dedicated, yet who are not going to take away any of his limelight). Also very important is the smoothness and charm he is capable of exuding when necessary. This is invaluable for recruiting quality athletes and alumni support. But I think above all what probably separates him from less successful coaches is his superior ability to play on the fears of boys in their late adolescence. Their fears of masculinity, their fears of acceptance, their fears of not being good enough—in short, their need to feel like acceptable men. Most of us had grown up to feel that being an adequate male had something to do with strength and proving ourselves. Football had been so important—made us stars and defined us— that this is where we believed we were to be judged. It would have been so much simpler to have a rite of passage into manhood with objective measurable tests that, once passed, were over. But instead, we could be made to feel like a man one day then a failure and loser the next. Even if we were stars our status was never certain. We could become losers overnight. We were trying to prove ourselves as men and we wanted approval from an authority that we'd passed the test. And Royal held the cards of approval; he knew what buttons to push, and he could take this approval away anytime by simply ignoring or banishing us.

He knew when to say "good job" and when to chew us
out and humble us in front of teammates. He could make
any of us totally ashamed simply by running the film projector back and forth, back and forth, never saying a single
word as the projector glared with our missed block. He was
always the judge and evaluator, detached and above. He
would often tell us when someone quit that if anyone else
was tired of it and wanted to quit, didn't want to pay the
price, then they should leave. But unspoken was what we
all felt, and we knew that to quit was to give in and admit
we couldn't cut it.

If you want to consider Royal's ability to get what he was
after, then he got his victories and titles and you would have
to judge him a success. But if you want to use other measures, like the effects he had on us as real human beings
and the concern he had for us as people as opposed to
trophies, and his help in making most of us healthier, hap-
pier, better off than before, I would have to judge him a
failure—and a big one. It's not that I think he was ma-
levolent, but just that his interests were not our interests.
To get what he wanted we were necessary means, but never
ends. Here, as he would say, actions speak louder than
words, and his actions belie any of his words of interest in
developing our character, etc., etc., etc. But his real failing
is not being able to see the power and effect of his actions
on the young males under him.

I think the kind of feeling Royal really had for us is best
exemplified by a statement he made to me my third spring.
I had started off spring training on the sixth team, but had
worked my way up to second-team guard and was challenging Danny Abbott for a first-team slot. We were blocking on dummies as Royal approached our drill. It was my

turn and I really popped the dummy making a nice hard sound.

Daddy D said simply, "Shaw, if you keep playing like that, we might have to start treating you like a white man around here." Then he turned and walked to another drill.

The Confrontation

Many would be cowards if they had courage enough.

Thomas Fuller, M.D.
GNOMOLOGIA (1732)

At the end of spring practice my third year, I was listed second team behind Danny Abbott in the *Texas Football* pre-season magazine, yet it was now clear in my mind that I wanted to be something more than a football player.

I came back to fall practice of my fourth year without the "psyche"—I just couldn't get it up. I was no longer fighting the fact that I didn't want to play. In fact, I was becoming increasingly aware of how I hated all of it, how much I felt trapped. And more than ever, I wanted to break loose.

We were just three days into fall training when my new apathy led to a confrontation. I obviously lacked my old fanaticism, and Coach Willie Zapalac (offensive line coach) was beginning to ride me. On the third morning of two-a-days, he was conducting offensive agility drills for the linemen. The particular drill was called the "monkey roll." It involved three players jumping over each other from a position on their hands and feet (four-point stance), rolling on the ground, then regaining their four-point position. Coach Zapalac became incensed that I wasn't rolling fast enough and pulled me by the jersey, jerking me up to his face. While holding me he said, "Son, I never want to see you loaf again. Is that clear?!"

Then after workout was over he came up to me and, grabbing me by the arm, repeated, "Son, if you ever loaf on me again, I'll kick your ass all over this field."

I was looking away from him this whole time. Then he started screaming that I'd better be listening to him and kept repeating, "Do you hear me, son! Do you hear me?"

To which I responded, "Yeah, I hear you." "Well, you'd better hear me because if you come out this afternoon [this was morning] and do the same thing I'm going to kick your butt off this field."

He had been holding me, and when he'd finished he pushed me away and told me to get into the field house. Anger was so tightly wrapped around my body I could hardly walk. All the way back to the dorm I thought about it. After lunch I couldn't get it out of my mind. I tried to sleep, but my heart was pounding through my head. Finally, I said to myself, "This is it. They aren't getting away with this. This afternoon I'm going to explode. When it comes time for agility drills and the monkey roll, I'm just going to lie there. And when Zapalac touches me, I'm going to let him have it."

My fantasy was that I'd kick his butt, throw off my head gear, sling my shoulder pads across the field, throw my shoes away, and then look up at that tower and give Royal the middle finger with both hands. I'd scream out "Fuck all this shit," and then walk off the field. I'd then go down and file assault charges on Zapalac if he'd laid a hand on me. This was to be the culmination of all that frustration, all those years of worrying if I was performing well enough, all that shit I'd been carrying. I was so nervous, anxious, and excited at these thoughts that I couldn't even sit down. I got up and started pacing the room. I began to get queasy. What would my teammates think? What would I tell my parents? What about my friends? What would it be like when I walked off that field?

The nervousness turned to trembling and I had to leave the dorm, so I went down by the practice field and walked along the creek that runs on one side. I was full of fear, but my thoughts were mostly about what I'd already left on that field the past three years. I was resolved and I knew what I was going to do and in my gut I felt no one could stop me—and if Zapalac kicked me as he'd promised, I would attack. Getting dressed for the workout, I was shaking. I'd told no one what my plans were, and felt completely alone. I felt it to be a huge daring revolt and the repercussions seemed almost unthinkable.

When I first saw Coach Zapalac, I felt physically weak. Then, in line waiting for my turn at the monkey roll, I wanted to vomit. But as my turn came I just lay down and stopped and waited . . . and waited . . . silence. Then Zapalac said in a very ordinary voice. "All right, men, next drill; guards over here with me, tackles go to Coach Manley." I lay there what seemed a full minute in stunned disbelief. He hadn't done anything—he'd even pretended not to notice, as if we hadn't even had our conversation that morning.

As I looked up into the Texas sun my body felt like slowly melting ice, and this watery letdown was indescribable. Again, I felt at a complete loss to act. In a certain sense there was relief, but far greater was the overwhelming feeling of disappointment. He'd known when to stop—he knew exactly what I was doing, and just removed himself.

Five minutes into the next drill I sustained a separated shoulder. The shoulder was to keep me out for two months, but I was now at the point of thinking it a lucky break. I had never felt farther from football.

This fourth fall I had moved away from the Tejas Club into another new setting—called College House—in a continuing effort to further disentangle myself from my narrow, jock world. College House was an apartment setting sponsored by the Ford Foundation and was supposed

to provide an intellectual atmosphere outside the classroom. It was composed of political radicals, hippies and
the drug culture, a few intellectuals, and many who were
simply lost. But one thing all residents had in common
was a basically negative attitude toward football and football players.

This was the fall of 1966 and political radicals were
fast becoming celebrities and a new campus force. But to
most in Moore-Hill this new breed of students was completely weird and strangely threatening. Not only was this
alien life style spreading, but football players were beginning to lose their role as campus heroes—so most jocks
passionately despised both political radicals and hippies,
though they didn't distinguish between the two. However,
I thought of myself as different from other jocks—more
curious and open, and I was determined to experience this
new world for myself.

Yet I was totally unprepared for my reception. I still
wore conservative clothes, spoke jock slang, had short
hair, and didn't mess with drugs. This, combined with the
fact that I was a football player, made me an automatic
zero in most of their eyes. I was stereotyped as "jock"—
except now it meant complete negativity. This was a jolt-
ing first for me, but I responded in typical winner fashion.
I decided to be the best at their own games—get the right
clothes and LP's, alter my slang, and move straight to the
top. "Yow, I'll beat those hippies at their own game."

But after an incident in my first week there, I knew I
wasn't any higher than seventh team. This notable event
occurred after a College House meeting with all of us,
thirty-five to forty, crowded into the apartment courtyard.
Instead of splitting up, everyone decided to play volleyball
and listen to music. Now at Moore-Hill we listened to

Johnny Cash, and about as far out as I ever got was the
Supremes. So when someone turned up his stereo full blast
with Bob Dylan screeching his *115th Dream,* I spontaneously and immediately screamed in my most powerful
jock voice, "Goddamn, what is that shit?"

Instant silence. For what seemed a full minute this
group of forty said nothing. I didn't know for sure what
sin I'd committed, but I knew I wasn't winning. And
quickly my efforts to reach the top of this group ended.

I had not been working out, and for all practical pur-
poses I was out of football. For the first time the people
around me were not only disinterested in football, they
were also not interested in my A's or lays. The competition was greatly minimized, and where it existed the rules
were uncertain and vague. I was lost. I made a brief effort
to be Plato's ideal man—the intellectual jock—by gob-
bling as much serious literature as I could find. But I
quickly despaired when I realized that I wasn't going to
be a number one philosopher in any short time, no matter
how frantic my effort.

With no goals and no place to go, years of despair
began introducing themselves. First cutting classes . . .
then tests . . . then school altogether. Drunk on week-
ends . . . every other night . . . every night. Up till two
A.M. playing cards and sleeping till noon . . . then four
A.M. and sleeping till two in the afternoon—then drink all
night . . . sleep all day. Seeing Tejas friends and a few
players . . . then no one. Finally—rarely leaving my small
room.

At just this low point I was scheduled to see the team
doctor about my shoulder. He examined it and informed
me that I could now go back to workouts. But even in my
depressed state I knew I didn't want to go back. There

were only three games left in the season and I knew that
I'd be nothing but a "blue marauder" again—a blocking
dummy. I decided I'd had it and I would tell Royal I was
through. This thought surprised me with its feelings of
strength and helped chase my despair. Suddenly I had the
sure sensation that this was what I must do and afterwards
things would somehow get better.

Going to see Coach Royal, I practiced what I would
say in a firm full voice—no hedging, no backing down—
and fought some obnoxious inner noise that laughed *Quitter, quitter, quitter, goddamned quitter.* "To hell with it—
I'm quitting—I tried; What more am I supposed to do?
That goddamned Royal doesn't give a shit about me. Why
should I be afraid of what he thinks—screw him." *Quitter
—quitter.*

"Mrs. Rhodes, I'd like to see Coach Royal," and immediately I was pissed at myself as I already felt like the
truant schoolboy. But before I could finish the self-lecture,
"Coach Royal can see you now—you can go on in," she
said.

Royal's office is thickly carpeted and his desk and chair
seem slightly elevated. As I sat down in the chair facing
him, I had to look up. Behind him was pictured a longhorn steer. The office was plush, like the kind corporation
presidents are supposed to have.

"Gary, what can I do for you?" And he leaned back in
his chair, hands behind his head, a pleasant calm look on
his face.

"Well, Coach . . . I saw the doctor yesterday and . . .
[yow] . . . and he said I could . . . work out again.
But . . . well, I just don't see any need of my going out
there again with only a few weeks left in the season."

His chair came solidly down, the hands left his head, the

smile vanished, and then his shoulders suddenly shot across the table—the only thing separating us. The suddenness shocked me and my recoiling neck was held in the room only by tense back muscles. His eyes were through me and he had the look of someone who wants to set the record straight.

"Don't you think that's our decision to make?"—said without a real question mark. "I'll decide whether there's any need or not, and we need people to run the other team's offense. We didn't put all that money in you to have you come tell me what you're going to do. *I* make those decisions. I expect you suited up tomorrow afternoon."

My built-in reaction was embarassment. How could I have considered saying what I did? "Yes, sir."

Then thirty minutes after the shock—anger—anger at myself for backing down—and disappointment.

I didn't sleep at all that night, and walking across campus to workout the next day I was planning some kind of dramatic rebellion on the field. It was two-thirty; a pretty afternoon and most people were in class, when crossing in front of the gymnasium I ran into Coach Royal. He smiled and walked toward me.

"Hi, Gary—where are you going?"

Stunned at his congeniality, I whispered, "To work out."

"Look Gary, we have enough men right now and there are just a couple of weeks left in the season. No use in your going down. We'll call you if we need you."

I couldn't understand it but tears filled my eyes and I felt remorse. "Coach, I'm sorry . . . sorry that I couldn't have done more for the team. I really wish I had . . ."

"Well, you were injured—it's just part of the game."

At a total loss for the words that would fit my feelings,

I repeated, "Thank you, Coach . . . I really enjoyed it
—just wish I could have . . . done more."

With that he smiled and walked away. As I turned to go
the other direction, I couldn't understand why I had to
cry.

A Beginning

Smart lad, to slip betimes away
From fields where glory does not stay
And early though the laurel grows
It withers quicker than the rose.

—from "To an Athlete Dying Young"
A. E. Housman

Three days after seeing Daddy D, I contacted a Navy recruiter. Even though I was a senior and near graduation, I felt like quitting the whole scene. It was partly a desire to complete what I had begun; if I was a quitter, then I would be a complete quitter. And it was also a desire to break cleanly with the past.

I had not been the son who revolts against papa's wishes and then dramatically leaves home, or even the son roundly kicked out. My departure was quiet, with Daddy D in control to the end. He hadn't really cared whether I came back to practice or not. What he had objected to was that I had taken some initiative in determining this for myself. He saw this as his natural prerogative, and there was no questioning his authority in such matters.

A couple of weeks before I planned to sign with the Navy, I began an endless series of long walks. On many of these, my roommate and close friend, Randy Boykin, joined me. We talked about the Navy (which eventually neither of us joined), school, and the future. On those chilly, clear fall nights some sort of rearrangement was taking place. For mostly unexplainable reasons, helped by the warmth of a friend, a sense of optimism was breaking from the neon lights of Austin streets. I finally decided to remain in school, and yet I had the distinct feeling of being on a new course.

The guilt and anxiety of quitting football were growing into a firm resentment, a clear hate of what I'd seen the past four years. It was a resentment that touched some inner base. I wanted to act.

Chachie and I started talking to each other several times a week. On each occasion we discussed football and what it had demanded of us. Our thoughts crystallized rapidly and we took turns attacking the abuses and hypocrisy of college football. I became incensed as I recalled some of the personal scenes I'd witnessed on a football field, the total disregard by the coaches of us as people, the complete sham of portraying us as student-athletes to the public, and the psychological misery we'd gone through and seen our friends go through. What could we do? We decided we couldn't let it go any further.

One November night in 1966 at two in the morning, Chachie woke me with an excited rap on my window.

"I've got it, I've got it!" he said.

"What are you talking about?"

"I've got it! I know what we're going to do."

"What are you talking about?"—and I was already up and getting dressed.

"Come out here!"—Chachie speaking in an excited whisper.

"What, goddamnit, what?" I could barely wait.

"We're going to do an exposé! We're going to tell all! We're going to have a news conference and let everyone know about shit drills and everything else that goes on!"

"Exposé?! News conference?! When? Where? What? How? Wow!"

"Shit yes!—and Shaw, we might even get a magazine to write about it. And they'll have to have investigations. Hell, this thing might even get on TV! Shaw, we're going to expose this shit and clean it up."

The rest of the night we walked and talked, mapping out our strategy. We would get other Texas players to go along, we would talk to professors, to doctors; why, even

get players from other schools in on it because we knew
the same thing went on at all big-time football schools. The
exhilaration of finally striking back was overwhelming.
The next day we went to work.

My first task was to talk to professors. I compiled a list
of who I thought were the fifteen most influential teachers
on campus. I set up appointments and talked to most of
them for well over an hour. Nearly all were responsive,
and increasingly I was recognizing that I did have a legiti-
mate right to object to these kinds of abuses. But I also
found nearly all of them to be pessimistic. They said we
were striking at something too powerful to touch. They
wished me luck, but doubted I would have any success.
The most pointed comments were made by Dr. John Silber,
then chairman of the philosophy department, now president of Boston University. He first said that he was pleasantly shocked that any football players would be attempting
such a thing; secondly, that we would have to be totally
prepared to be able to fully document all charges to have
any effect; and thirdly, we were taking severe risks. "You
better get at least three crackerjack lawyers. You're fighting the real powers of this state. Erwin won't let you get
past first base." Frank Erwin is the most powerful member
of the Texas University Board of Regents and was, until recently, its chairman. He has long had political ties with Connally and Johnson (he was chairman of Texas' National
Democratic delegation), and it is his political strength that
is considered the principal reason that Texas University
gets a great proportion of the state's educational funds. He
has ruled the university with an iron fist, and his tremendous power has resulted in the departure of several of the
University's most prominent professors. "If they don't like
it, they can leave." When it comes to sports and educa-

tion, Erwin has said, "I want a university the football team can be proud of." Indeed, it was not uncommon to see certain football players riding around the campus in Erwin's orange (Texas Orange) cadillac.] "And you better have mimeographed copies of the medical records with the football injuries you speak of because you will find that they will mysteriously disappear. And most importantly, you must realize you're putting yourself in possible physical danger." I couldn't help smiling at these statements since I thought them ridiculously exaggerated, if not paranoid.

After talking to the professors, we talked to a few other players. We found that even those "successful," that is, starters, were very sympathetic and on most particular aspects fully agreed with us. Yet there was an extreme reluctance on their part to be part of anything public. They preferred to keep their "bitches" to themselves. There were a thousand and one reasons given, but I felt there were generally two main reasons for this reluctance: one was plain fear of the consequences, the other was that, although they agreed that there were the abuses and depersonalization, they still clung to the basic tenets of the system. They could not disentangle themselves or realize that these tenets and their acceptance were the very things that led to the abuses and depersonalization. Still we did find several who agreed to participate if there were enough others involved. But we stopped this approach when we realized that talking to other players would have to be last on the agenda if we had any hopes of keeping it secret until we were ready. So we stopped after talking to eight players.

At this point I contacted a state legislator whom I'd known for several years. I asked him about the possibilities of government investigation and legislation. He, of course, told us that any state legislator who tried to involve himself in that kind of investigation would be "crucified." But he did put us in touch with a Dallas public relations man who had close contacts in the important news media. We talked to him and he went to work. He contacted *Sports Illustrated, Look,* and *Life,* among others. *Sports Illustrated* said "it was too hot." *Look* had to think about it. *Life* sent their sports editor, Jack McDermott, down from New York. We met him in Houston. Chachie and I were in a trance. *Life* magazine! After we spent several hours with McDermott, he was enthusiastic and definitely interested. After a couple of weeks of consultation and correspondence, they were ready to go ahead. They even suggested to us that they thought it would be a big story, and that they had tentative plans for making it a cover story the following September when the next football season opened! In just three months Chachie and I were now talking about the cover of *Life* magazine. We were ecstatic.

But things did not go smoothly with *Life.* We, of course, never knew the real story, but we did learn it concerned inter-office squabblings at some of the magazine's higher echelons. They decided to delay the whole project until the next year. As could have been expected, we heard less and less through the next six months and the project died a slow nagging death.

Yet even as the *Life* failure became imminent and the fever of vendetta subsided, I moved toward the core of my rebellion. With the affirmation of Chachie and a few faculty members, I was no longer denying my own feelings of anger and resentment. For the first time I not only accepted my defiance, I welcomed it. In fact, I trusted these feelings as I had trusted nothing else in my four years under Daddy D.

But after the *Life* project had passed, I didn't know

what else to do with these new feelings of rebellion. Within a few months I began to lose my resentment. Instead, I drifted towards listlessness. I began frequently fantasizing about my Texas football career and periodically I had thoughts of great redemption. In between these daydreams I tried to decide what I wanted to do. I had no idea.

After I graduated and flunked my army physical (the army doctor decided I did have a small hole in my heart after all) I spent the next two months doing nothing. Economic necessity moved me into a series of odd jobs: waiter, fireman, security guard, and educational research assistant. The last one took me to California.

In California, a thousand miles from Texas, I began for the first time to feel truly removed from the coaches—from their rules, their controls, their whole world-view. And the result was something both totally unexpected and totally predictable: I began to have sharp anxiety attacks, accompanied by a sense of imminent disaster. I found it impossible to imagine myself in the future and feelings of an empty past became acute. This anxiety was only temporarily relieved by constructing artificial challenges. I would concentrate on losing weight—at one time I managed to get down to 170. Or I'd juggle my finances—repeatedly refiguring how I would eliminate my small school debts and save money at the same time. Another favorite was getting in shape. I would work up to running so many miles a day while systematically improving my time. Each of these obsessive pursuits touched my old football world of self-denial and discipline, and they at least provided some familiarity.

Finally, I decided that my only remedy was to choose a firm goal, a career. I hoped that once I had determined this, my sense of impending doom would disappear. My newly chosen goal was graduate school and I returned to Austin in the spring of 1969 to begin.

After I had been back in Texas six months the intensity of my needs finally overpowered my fear of personal involvement. I went way past my five-date rule.

Carolyn had a gentle softness that made it seem easy to let go. After only two weeks we were seeing each other every day. Within a month I had a feeling of being saved. For the first time in my life I felt real intimacy. The three months that followed far surpassed anything I'd known. And at times even the future seemed pleasantly irrelevant. I couldn't imagine why I'd denied myself so long. In fact, for weeks I indulged in sex, food, fun, and warm feelings. Carolyn and I were constantly together.

Then seemingly for no reason my acute anxiety returned. At first it came only in brief periods. Then as my feelings for Carolyn deepened, these periods expanded and became more intense. Our closeness left me with a vague feeling of some ultimate failure. I even felt that something horrible was about to happen. Somehow I was going to lose everything. And with only meager trust in my own senses, I began to grab for rules and regulations. How do I know if I love her? How much should I love her? What should I do if I love her? This need for programmed control led me to the old question of measuring up—coming through in the big game. The "right" development of our relationship became another ultimate test of my manhood and worth. And self-doubts about blowing it were followed by increased efforts to manage my feelings. In turn, this disciplined control put distance between us. This distance pulled together an already tense apprehension. I feared losing her. Soon I was frantically trying to deny all my emotions. But it was hard to cover my deep feelings for Carolyn—and finally a life of control became too much.

I checked into the psychiatric ward of the student health center. The previous night I had been afraid to go to sleep. I couldn't let go enough to close my eyes—it was too threatening. For three days I couldn't keep still. I crossed my arms, held my shoulders, and kept moving. In those three days I lost thirteen pounds.

A few times in my two week stay I managed to relax my rigid control. The difference was that this time it was with an awareness that basically my misery was due to this control—not the lack of it. What I had been avoiding in California was a beginning—not some horrible end.

In these last several years I have found that separating myself from others' rules, and learning to live by my own feelings takes time and effort. When I'd first experienced a free-flow of feeling with Carolyn, I had come alive. But past a certain point this new sense of relying on my own feelings was disorienting and frightening. My response was to frantically grab for more rules. This, it seems to me, is the crux of the big-time football player's predicament. All of his values, his reactions, his ways of measuring himself as a man, were given to him. So here is his dilemma: If he clings to these criteria, he's headed for a narrow constricting life based on some masculine myth about winning; and if he cuts loose, rejects the values, the rules, the measures that he's built his whole life on up to that point, he's at a complete and painful loss. In a sense, the meaning has been taken from his life, and listlessness and anxiety are all but inevitable.

It's a jeopardy that's not restricted to football players. The combat veteran who leaves the army, the person who leaves his religion, the long-term prisoner getting out of

jail—anybody whose whole set of rigidly determined values
and performances are taken away—they are all at the same
kind of loss. The big time athlete needs rehabilitation every
bit as much as these. And it takes time. You try to just walk
away from all the old values of your life and you find yourself backsliding often, reaching out for some new rigidity—
something you can cling to. Finding a new way of life in
which I depend on my own feelings and not on someone
else's goals has been the most important thing I've learned
to do since leaving football.

During this time I have come to see that resentment and
rebellion were beginnings of this self-expression, but they
were only the first step. When I initially revolted against
Royal's system, I was revolting in the way lowly Baylor rose
up to knock off Texas. To a large degree my worth was
still dependent on Royal's response to my revolt. I was
similar to an adolescent boy who rebels against his father,
yet is obviously very dependent on his father's acknowl-
edgment and response to his rebellion.

Silber had been right. It was not easy. But now I knew the
extent of the problem was far deeper than exposing the
abuses of college football. I also realized that Silber had
not been paranoid about the connections between Royal,
Connally and Erwin. (Silber was fired three years later by
Erwin in a supposed disagreement over departmental re-
organization.) They were more than coincidental.

It's not just that football is so popular and that attacking
it would endanger the enjoyment these people have on
Saturday afternoons. And it runs much deeper than the
fact that football is a big business, and big businessmen
happen to like one another's company. No, I think it runs
right to the core of the American psyche. These big shots
are all "winners" whose most basic tenet is the same as the

motivational core of football. Only a few get to be winners, and you make it by competing and by defeating others. Life is a big football game. It's why politicians like Nixon praise football so much. It's why Nixon loves to be thought of as the quarterback, and why he constantly reminds us of his losing in 1960, and then "fighting back" to defeat Humphrey in 1968—thus proving his worth as a winner. To attack football is to attack the major exhibit of the masculine view of the world. And on a gut level, the winners in this survival-of-the-fittest code sense the connection. Thus to condemn the method of college football would be to condemn their simplistic world view and focus light on the shallow, deprived existence that depends on glory, fame, and power. It would be much more strongly resisted than an attack on the church or most other American institutions (if not all) because the football code is much more their lifeblood, and their lifeblood in its purest, most elemental form. It is a lifeblood that they accurately sense is already being eroded by youth and the new culture. So these relationships of power—Royal, Connally, and Erwin —and their connections to American football are not casual. Football is the strongest remaining unquestioned remnant of an old culture, and the struggle to change its current form is no less than the conflict between an old culture and a new culture.

Philip Slater says in *The Pursuit of Loneliness* that if change does not affect the motivational roots of a society then it is not real change. The development of a cooperative society where individual worth and strength is not based on defeating others cannot be accomplished by using the old culture's rules. To concentrate on competing against and defeating those in power is to replace one winner with another. Instead we must use our energies to discover our real wants and then move toward fulfilling them. In the process, we will obviously come into conflict with parts of the old culture, but then we can deal with these difficulties as part of the larger problem of becoming more fully human. At this moment our main concentration is on conquering this culture, but we are keeping the old culture's principal motivational tenet. So the biggest danger in eliminating our football mentality is in using its very values to eliminate only the "game."

Certainly for blacks, students, and increasingly for members of the middle class, resistance to external dominance and control is an important beginning toward change and independence. But this self-affirmation cannot live long with rebellion as its only expression. It remains narrow and limited if it never expands past a winner-loser mentality because, more than anything else, it is this winner mentality and its disguised elitism that permeates American life, be it pursuing the elusive and exclusive romantic dream girl (or boy), striving for the presidency of your business, struggling for the top economic level or getting the Ph.D. that scores your final touchdown in school. All these are part of making the "first team," and for most of us they run roughshod over the needs of community that lie below them. These touchdowns are so frantically pursued because they are means of convincing ourselves that we are members of an elite winner. Depending on your particular group, the lesser losers can be "rednecks," "niggers," "commies," the silent majority, the radical left, anybody that doesn't have a college degree, anyone that does, anybody making less than $20,000, anyone making more than $20,000, anyone for a revolution, anyone who opposes one—*ad nauseam*. And generations of Americans have kept believing just one more victory will win peace and democracy. Even now, our national quarterback, Nixon, calls for a fresh bombing assault on North Vietnam, naming it "Operation Linebacker." And just as traditionally American a part of the counterculture believes revolution and final victory over American imperialism will lead to some Nirvana.

Unfortunately, rooting out this compulsive need to win is a slow process, and in the years since Daddy D I've often failed to avoid its web.

Yet, ever increasingly I have found experiences that go beyond victory. In fact, I've found that some of these possibilities exist in sports. An example of this is the moment on a football field that for me soars above all others. It happened five full years after my last Texas workout.

My life-long friend, Dee Wilson, and I frequently spent our late summer afternoons running pass patterns and playing touch football. Some days I would be the quarterback and Dee the receiver, and on others it was vice versa. One September day we were playing two other friends on the otherwise empty field of a high school stadium. We were in good shape and had been playing for almost two hours. But now all of us were tired and it was getting dark, so we agreed the next play would be our last. Dee and I had been working on one pass pattern for a couple of days, and though it had been unsuccessful that afternoon, we had decided to try it again on this final play. What followed was an experience I'd never had before.

At the end of this pattern, Dee was to be about thirty yards downfield angling for the corner of the end zone. But as I dropped back and pointed my eyes toward his full strides into late afternoon, I began to feel some inexplicable postponement of time. My mind was quick and clear, yet all physical movement fell into a lingering genus of departure. With a sudden calmness, I could see the whole field and the three small figures elegantly brushing its top. As I watched their grace, I could feel the empty stands and their suspension of a lost past. This changeless spell brought an acute sense of temporalness and the feeling of inevitably fading with the dusk. Yet just as acute was the sense that this present intimately belonged to both past and future. This time and our movements were one. As I released the ball with the giving length and completeness of my arm, I could see the beginning of its easy soft arc. And it somehow seemed perfectly coordinated with the stadium, the ground, early evening and the four of us. As the ball was coming down some thirty long yards into the distance, two figures in ballet stretched into the air to meet it. In one easy motion of symmetry, Dee took the pass and lissomely yielded to a surging turf. Then slowly and gently separating himself from the stadium ground, he turned to me and grinned. I knew we had connected.

Author's Note

The writing and research of this book was made possible in part by a grant from the Institute for the Study of Sport and Society. In addition to this financial aid, Jack and Micki Scott, directors of the Institute, gave me much emotional and intellectual support. I suggest that the Institute be the focal point for everyone working toward the humanization of sports in the seventies. The Institute for The Study of Sport and Society is now located at Oberlin College; Oberlin, Ohio.

—Gary Shaw